W9-BRY-177

What people are saying about …

MAKING MARRIAGE BEAUTIFUL

"With careful precision, Dorothy Greco examines the complexities, pain, and beauty inherent in our marriages and guides us chapter by hope-filled chapter into the wisdom needed to cultivate marriages that overflow with love and beauty."

Marlena Graves (married 16 years),
author of *A Beautiful Disaster*

"A remarkably honest and profoundly wise road map for real marriage—the kind that survives relational ups and downs, twists and turns, and disappointments and doubts long enough to become a beautiful reflection of the life-changing, love-giving Christ. Greco paints this real-marriage landscape with uncanny skill, deft insight, and fearless power. Five stars!"

Patricia Raybon (married 41 years), award-winning
author of *I Told the Mountain to Move* and *Undivided*

"Dorothy Greco offers deep yet extremely practical ways to build a Christ-honoring, thriving relationship. This book will speak life-changing truth straight into the heart of your marriage."

Jeffrey P. Bjorck, PhD (married 26 years),
psychology professor at Fuller Theological
Seminary and licensed psychologist

"*Making Marriage Beautiful* is full of goodness and truth, and is one of the wisest and most comprehensive books on marriage I've ever read."

Karen Swallow Prior, PhD (married 31 years),
author of *Booked* and *Fierce Convictions*

"I tend to avoid marriage books. Often, their idealism sends me into the sloughs of 'guilt' and 'despond.' Not Greco's book. She offers an honest, literate, and biblical marriage playbook that is as inspiring as it is doable. Because of this lovely book, I'll be looking for outbursts of beauty in marriages everywhere. Even in mine."

Leslie Leyland Fields (married 39 years),
author of *Crossing the Waters*

"*Making Marriage Beautiful* is a unique, remarkably engaging, and vulnerable treatise. It shows me how, even after thirty-one years of marriage, I've got more to learn."

Rev. Ray Kollbocker (married 31 years),
the senior pastor of Parkview Community
Church in Glen Ellyn, IL

"This book is honest, humbly written, and wise. Rather than formulas or edicts, Greco has given us a gospel-centered theology and ethic of Christian marriage. But it's about more than marriage—ultimately it's about the good news that Jesus rescues and transforms sinners like you and me."

Amy Simpson (married 23 years), inner
strength coach and author of *Anxious*

"Greco uses her brilliance as a writer and a creative wordsmith to convey a winsome and challenging message about marriage. This is just not 'another book on Christian marriage.' This is a must-read for anyone wishing to gain insight and instruction on their marriage journey."

Dr. Virginia Friesen (married 40 years), author of *Raising a Trailblazer* and coauthor of *The Marriage App*

"*Making Marriage Beautiful* offers readers a wise book that veers wide of clichéd fixes. Dorothy Greco tackles the kinds of issues that sabotage real relational growth. This book will benefit newlyweds as well as couples who've been together for decades."

Michelle Van Loon (married 37 years), author of *Moments & Days*

"Dorothy Greco's wise and pastoral book offers probing questions at the end of each chapter, which I particularly like. These questions (and this book) will be a tool for self-understanding, spiritual formation, and by God's grace, marital growth."

Jen Pollock Michel (married 20 years), author of *Teach Us to Want* and *Keeping Place*

"With humor, warmth, and honesty, Greco calls us to be not only better spouses but better individuals and better followers of Jesus."

Dorcas Cheng-Tozun (married 11 years), Inc.com columnist and *Christianity Today* contributor

"Dorothy Greco has generously opened her heart and her marriage for us to mine her hard-won wisdom. Her gospel-centered perspective combined with real stories of couples makes me recommend this book to anyone who longs to build a beautiful marriage!"

Suzanne Burden (married 8 years), coauthor of *Reclaiming Eve* and pastor

"Dorothy Greco wades into a myriad of marriage challenges with a candid discussion of her own marriage. Readers who long for a stronger, more meaningful marriage partnership will find plenty of wisdom, help, and encouragement here."

Carolyn Custis James (married 36 years), author of *Half the Church* and *Malestrom*

"Dorothy's smart and sensitive words direct me to Jesus for grace and offer tools and testimonies to spur me on to love my wife better."

Andrew Comiskey (married 35 years), pastor and author of *Strength in Weakness*

"Dorothy Greco invites us to see how marital challenges become invitations for spiritual transformation."

Kelli Trujillo (married 17 years), editor of *Christianity Today*

"Dorothy Greco brings a refreshing female voice to the marriage conversation: candid, thoughtful, wise, and well researched, with helpful examples from actual marriages, including her own. A solid resource for couples, pastors, and congregations."

Sarah Arthur (married 16 years), coauthor of *The Year of Small Things*

"Dorothy has done us all a great service by inviting us into her marriage journey with insight and courage. Christopher's vulnerability and stories make this book *required reading* for men who want to experience deeper delight in their marriage."

Brian Doerksen (married 32 years), pastor, worship leader, and songwriter

"In *Making Marriage Beautiful*, Dorothy Greco offers a grace-filled, clear-minded, and motivating look at modern marriage."

Andrea Palpant Dilley (married 11 years), contributing editor of *Christianity Today*

MAKING

MARRIAGE

LIFELONG LOVE, JOY, AND INTIMACY
START WITH YOU

DOROTHY LITTELL GRECO

with contributions from CHRISTOPHER GRECO

David C Cook®
transforming lives together

MAKING MARRIAGE BEAUTIFUL
Published by David C Cook
4050 Lee Vance Drive
Colorado Springs, CO 80918 U.S.A.

David C Cook U.K., Kingsway Communications
Eastbourne, East Sussex BN23 6NT, England

The graphic circle C logo is a registered trademark of David C Cook.

The website addresses recommended throughout this book are offered as a
resource to you. These websites are not intended in any way to be or imply an
endorsement on the part of David C Cook, nor do we vouch for their content.

Details in some stories have been changed to protect the identities of the persons involved.

Unless otherwise noted, all Scripture quotations are taken from the *Holy Bible*, New
Living Translation, copyright © 1996, 2007 by Tyndale House Foundation. Used by
permission of Tyndale House Publishers, Inc., Carol Stream, Illinois 60188. All rights
reserved. Scripture quotations marked KJV are taken from the King James Version of the
Bible. (Public Domain.); TLB are taken from The Living Bible, copyright © 1971. Used
by permission of Tyndale House Publishers, Inc., Carol Stream, Illinois 60188. All rights
reserved; NIV are taken from the Holy Bible, NEW INTERNATIONAL VERSION®,
NIV®. Copyright © 1973, 2011 by Biblica, Inc.® Used by permission. All rights
reserved worldwide. NEW INTERNATIONAL VERSION® and NIV® are
registered trademarks of Biblica, Inc. Use of either trademark for the offering
of goods or services requires the prior written consent of Biblica, Inc.; NRSV are
taken from the New Revised Standard Version Bible, copyright 1989, Division
of Christian Education of the National Council of the Churches of Christ in
the United States of America. Used by permission. All rights reserved.
The author has added italics to Scripture quotations for emphasis.

LCCN 2016943744
ISBN 978-0-7814-1408-1
eISBN 978-1-4347-1000-0

© 2017 Dorothy Littell Greco
Published in association with the literary agency of Credo Communications, LLC,
Grand Rapids, Michigan, www.credocommunications.net.

The Team: Alice Crider, Amy Konyndyk, Nick Lee,
Cara Iverson, Abby DeBenedittis, Susan Murdock
Cover Design: Connie Gabbert

Printed in the United States of America
First Edition 2017

1 2 3 4 5 6 7 8 9 10

101416

To Mary, Kate, and all of my Redbud sisters:
Maybe it doesn't always take a
village, but it did this time.

To Christopher:
None of this would make any sense without you.
Thank you for letting me finish the hat.

CONTENTS

FOREWORD

When I got married, I gave little thought to how marriage might change me. The one exception was that I thought it would make me happier. I don't think it crossed my mind that God would use my marriage to make me more like Christ. I knew I had much room for spiritual growth, but I thought God's method would be Scripture and the convicting, empowering work of the Holy Spirit. I never thought He would reveal so many of my flaws through my marriage.

Having counseled couples over the last four decades, I have discovered that I am not the only one who has experienced this reality. The good news is that God changes hearts. When the attitude of Christ begins to consume us, we become the loving, supportive, caring people we thought we were in the beginning. It takes the challenges and the pain of marriage to reveal the truth: we are all sinners in the process of being redeemed.

In *Making Marriage Beautiful*, Dorothy Greco vulnerably shares the journey she and her husband have traveled through brokenness to beauty. Whether you are newly married, feeling the growing pains of middle age, or looking back over many decades together, you will find this book both inspiring and insightful. My prayer is that God will use *Making Marriage Beautiful* to encourage you and help you interpret the events of life from His perspective.

Gary D. Chapman, PhD, author
of The 5 Love Languages®

INTRODUCTION

God's will was for us to be made holy
by the sacrifice of the body of Jesus Christ, once for all time.
Hebrews 10:10

We are not yet what we shall be, but we are growing toward it.
The process is not yet finished, but it is going on.
This is not the end, but it is the road.
All does not yet gleam in glory, but all is being purified.
Martin Luther

I have two confessions to make.

I am not a marriage expert.

I do not have a perfect marriage.

So why would I spend a year of my life writing a marriage book? For two reasons. First, my husband, Christopher, and I agree that creating and sustaining a healthy marriage is one of the most challenging (and wonderful!) endeavors we have ever embarked upon. We know we're not outliers, because for the past twenty years, we have counseled, taught, and prayed with hundreds of other couples. During that time, we've witnessed how passionately they want their marriages to flourish and how overwhelmed and under-resourced they sometimes feel. Regardless of whether your marriage is thriving, struggling, or somewhere in between, we strongly believe there's no such thing as too much encouragement or wise counsel.

The second reason for writing this book is that we needed it. I started working on *Making Marriage Beautiful* during the most difficult season of our life together. Due to several crises (outside of our marriage), our world unraveled, leaving us angry, hurt, and confused. We prayed and processed for months but then began to feel increasingly numb and started retreating from everyone, including each other. In that fragile place, we sensed the Holy Spirit challenge us to renew our commitment to love.

Ultimately, what enabled us to obey God's directive during that destabilizing season was not our willpower, not some awesome conference, and definitely not our winsome personalities. It was our devotion to Jesus Christ and our desire to be saved.

Too often, Christians assume that salvation is a singular, defining event. This mentality may result in living our "entire life 'saved' but relatively unchanged."[1] As much as we might want it to be true, saying yes to Christ does not instantly eradicate all of our sin patterns and make us holy overnight. We *become* Christians in a process that begins the first time we turn our faces toward Him and ends the day He calls us home. Author and spiritual director Ruth Haley Barton describes this journey in *Life Together in Christ*:

> Salvation is not merely about knowing where we are going when we die; it is also about the possibility of kingdom living here and now. It is about

being fundamentally changed in the depths of
our being so that the will of God can be done *in
our lives* on earth as it is in heaven.

Spiritual transformation is the process by
which Christ is formed in us—for the glory of
God, for the abundance of our own lives and for
the sake of others.[2]

This process of being fundamentally changed and allowing
Christ to be formed in us should influence the nature of who we
are and then benefit every one of our relationships, first and foremost our marriages.

There are probably only a handful of times when we make an
earnest but innocent commitment that leads to radical transformation. One example is pledging our lives to Jesus and another is
pledging our lives to our spouses. Provided you have been married
for more than forty-eight hours, you know that marriage changes
you. We cannot expect two fully formed, egocentric adults to
suddenly occupy the same square footage without something
having to give. That something needs to be our immaturity and
self-centeredness, for marriage, according to author Mike Mason,
is "an unrelenting guerrilla war against selfishness." He says,

Amidst all our pleasant little fantasies of omnip-
otence and blamelessness and self-sufficiency,
marriage explodes like a bomb.... It attacks people's vanity and lonely pride in a way that few
other things can.[3]

As marriage attacks our vanity and pride, it beckons us to turn away from the mirror so we can move toward Christ and our spouses. Over time, the explosions diminish, the mirror becomes less compelling, and the turning becomes easier. The humbling yet glorious process of being transformed so that we can love is what this book is all about.

Christopher and I have always felt prompted by God to share our lives honestly and vulnerably. We do so not to draw attention to ourselves, but because we believe that telling our story reveals God's faithfulness, goodness, and mercy. To keep quiet is to deny His work in our lives.

That said, an inherent challenge in writing a marriage book, particularly an honest one, is that my spouse is coming along for the ride. It's one thing to write my story and quite another to write *our* story. I have not included any details or anecdotes without Christopher's blessing. So that you have a distinctly male perspective, his point of view and experiences are woven throughout the text. He shares some initial thoughts below:

> In a very real sense, nobody other than Christ taught us how to live out our lives together. No couple intentionally mentored us or helped us track our progress. This is a calling of the Lord—a vision of what marriage might look like if we regularly and humbly submit our hearts to Him and choose to grow.
>
> This book is not a statement that we know all there is to know about marriage. But this

much we do know: The Lord has honored our choices, exceeded our expectations, and revealed His attentive and compassionate presence to us during our darkest moments. This book is a gesture of thanks to Him and a fool's hope that it might serve others.

It's important for you to know that I wholeheartedly approve of everything Dorothy has written, even the places where she articulates my limitations. In fact, the parts of this book that make me laugh the hardest are where she precisely captures my foibles. We included many specific and vulnerable examples to make it clear that this book was written by real people in a real marriage.

(See why I love him?)

In Jen Pollock Michel's book, *Teach Us to Want*, she confesses, "My real trouble as a writer isn't trying to mean the words that I write; it's living into the words that I mean. Nonfiction writing can feel like the high art of hypocrisy."[4] Indeed. According to Christopher, "There are often cavernous and treacherous discrepancies between who we say we are and who we actually are, and nobody knows that better than our spouses." I am acutely aware that within any conversation about marriage lies the possibility of fraudulent claims and self-deceit. Every fight we had during the past year caused a tsunami of doubt to crash over me, making me question my integrity as well as my credentials.

In an attempt to check any hypocritical tendencies, after finishing each chapter, I asked myself two questions: *Were these concepts actually helping me love Christopher today? And, historically speaking, have they helped us and our marriage grow stronger and healthier?* The answer was always yes. Perhaps the real measure of this book's efficacy is that writing it actually helped me to become a better, more loving spouse. If you read it and apply the concepts, I believe the same will be true for you.

Making Marriage Beautiful will be relevant regardless of how long you have been married, your ethnicity, or your socioeconomic context. In the hope of representing the diverse world in which we live, I have interviewed eight couples from various ethnic backgrounds. Their names have been changed, but their stories have not been altered.

Though the best scenario would be to read this book with your spouse, it will be constructive even if only one of you is actively working on your marriage. I cannot guarantee that it will save a broken relationship, but I can guarantee that choosing to follow Jesus more intentionally will benefit you and your family.

At the end of each chapter, incisive questions will help you process and apply what you've read. The questions will also provide a starting point if you want to study this book with other couples. Additional resources, including suggestions for further reading, can be found on my website, www.dorothygreco.com.

Though it was not my intention when I started this project, about halfway through, I realized I was not simply crafting a book; I was also creating a prayer. For all of us. Please read the following pages with an open heart. Incline yourself in hope toward Christ and toward your spouse. Wait and see what the Lord will do. He is faithful and good. All the time.

MARRIAGE WILL CHANGE YOU

What Do You Want That Change to Look Like?

Christopher and I got divorced before we got married. Several months into our first engagement, he abruptly severed the relationship and refused to communicate with me, crushing any hope of reconciliation.

Two years passed. While typing a document at work, he had a seemingly random thought: *Maybe I made a mistake.* Not long after, he called me to ask if I would consider getting together to discuss what happened. Eight months later, he proposed a second time and I said yes again, to the consternation of many friends and family members.

As the wedding date drew near, the forecasts we received from these friends were soberingly consistent: "Be prepared. You guys are going to have a hard first year of marriage." They weren't aiming to discourage us. They had witnessed our tumultuous premarital relationship and knew us to be strong willed (read *obstinate*), articulate (*opinionated*), and determined (*inflexible*). Despite their well-grounded concerns, we did not cancel our nuptials. Nor did we forget their warnings.

After we officially became husband and wife, each minor disturbance caused us to hold our breath and scan the horizon for the predicted storms. Fortunately, our friends were wrong about year one. It wasn't until year ten that the tornado hit, but by that time our roots were deep enough to withstand the wind.

What gave us the courage to try again when the first version of our relationship ended so poorly? Though we had both been actively following Christ for nearly a decade, our breakup revealed a depth of brokenness and immaturity neither of us had been aware of. Instead of simply moving on or denying these painful revelations via numbing, self-deception, or blame, Christopher and I chose Jesus. As we regularly turned toward and embraced Christ, His unflinching love and steadfast faithfulness began to set us free. The slow and gradual transformation emboldened us to reengage and has subsequently resulted in a rich and satisfying marriage.

Not Even on the Radar

Because of my various vocational roles, which include lay pastor and professional photographer, I've officiated and photographed hundreds of brides and grooms as they promised to love, honor, and cherish each other. You have probably not witnessed as many weddings as I have, but perhaps you have also noticed that marriage vows lack specificity. How, exactly, are we supposed to love, honor, and cherish our imperfect spouses for the remainder of our lives?

During those giddy months leading up to our weddings, we tend to be so intoxicated by oxytocin-fueled love and so distracted by choosing the DJ, venue, and reception appetizers that we rarely dwell upon what it takes to execute these lofty promises. We assume the present euphoria will carry us through sickness and health, poverty and wealth, and everything else in between. If you have not already experienced this for yourself, based on twenty-five years of marriage and almost as many years supporting other couples, I can assure you that the prewedding bliss will dissipate, leaving you confused and disoriented. Those destabilizing feelings actually serve us because they reveal the truth that we need much more than strong emotions and good intentions to faithfully fulfill our vows.

Making a beautiful marriage depends on something seldom covered by premarital classes, which tend to focus on tangible concepts such as communication, in-laws, finances, and of course, sex. Marking these and other potentially hazardous areas with fluorescent orange spray paint is useful. It can prompt proactive conversations that will help us better understand one another and navigate our differences.

However, knowledge and navigational skills are not enough to get you to your tenth anniversary, let alone your silver. What differentiates a loving, joyful, intimate marriage from a disappointing, frustrating one is the willingness and commitment to be changed, to say yes to God's transforming work, and to become increasingly holy with each passing year.

Like It or Not, We Need to Be Willing to Acknowledge Our Sin

Oddly enough, we cannot move toward holiness unless we recognize and admit our sin. We dare not deny or be vague about that sin if our goal is to become more like Jesus Christ. Here's the challenge that all of us currently face: we live in a culture that discourages us from confessing and taking responsibility for our sin. To some extent, this has always been true (see Adam and Eve, Genesis 3), but it looks notably different now than it did just thirty to forty years ago, when I first decided to follow Jesus.

In the late seventies and early eighties, college students like me who believed in Jesus were encouraged to regularly share our faith with others. We approached total strangers, handed them a simplistic pamphlet, and proceeded to tell them that if they did not repent of their sin, they would be separated from God for all eternity. It was by no means subtle or culturally sensitive, but by God's grace it often resulted in lively conversations and the occasional spontaneous conversion. Today this approach would be judged as inappropriate, in part because our culture is much more sensitive to any dialogue that lacks nuance.

During the Cold War, nuance was not a national priority. Because we had recently participated in two horrific wars and continued to live under the looming threat of a nuclear apocalypse, we endeavored to protect ourselves by creating a binary world of good guys (those who practiced democracy) and bad guys (the Communists). Regardless of one's theological beliefs—or lack thereof—there was general agreement about mankind's depravity and life's fragility. Even the clergy shied away from nuance by emphasizing the destructive power of sin and the terrors of hell.

The winds of social change that were blowing in the nineties, when Communism crumbled, began howling at gale force by the beginning of the twenty-first century. Modernism's black-and-white framework was gradually replaced by postmodernism's fifty shades of gray. The shifting winds have deeply affected many aspects of the culture at large as well as individual expressions of faith. Those of you who are millennials typically have a thirst for justice (as demonstrated by the movement to end all forms of slavery), an inclination to share rather than own (think Zipcar), and a growing passion for protecting the environment—all outworkings of the desire for a more holistic lifestyle and a more integrated faith. These are welcome and needed corrections to the previous generations' sometimes disintegrated understanding of Christian life.

There is a hidden downside to the changing ideologies. Even though we now have a more robust picture of what our faith could look like, these seismic cultural shifts have pushed an essential component of Christ off to the side. The postmodern propensity toward tolerance, combined with every generation's avoidance of shame and responsibility, now inclines us toward a Messiah characterized predominantly by grace and mercy. Although these are both facets of Jesus, Scripture affirms that He also has a sword-like tongue and will judge us according to our deeds (Matt. 16:27; Rom. 2:5–10; Rev. 19:15).

Like everyone else, I prefer grace and mercy to judgment. But if we routinely dismiss or minimize our sin—for any reason—we have no impetus to change. This leaves our marriages vulnerable to failure. Jen Pollock Michel sagely writes, "Without the doctrine of sin, we are led toward being unusually optimistic about our humanity. We will refuse to face the viciousness of our capabilities and will trust our desires too much and fear ourselves too little."[1] Being mindful of our sin and how it affects others is not meant to crush or disempower us; it's meant to motivate us to be less self-centered and more Christ-centered.

Transformation Begins When We Admit Our Brokenness and Need

Shifting our center toward Jesus is not a onetime event; it's a process that begins when we acknowledge our need to be saved. As we make this life-changing confession, we recalibrate our internal GPS to Jesus. He becomes our "anthropological North Star,"[2] beckoning us toward Him and revealing our sin and brokenness in the process. Thankfully, as Jesus helps us to see those areas where we need redemption, He also invites us to lean on Him.

For those of you like me who prefer self-sufficiency over dependence, admitting need and allowing others to help creates tremendous disequilibrium. Because we have been hurt and disappointed so many times, it's terrifying to give up control and trust anyone—including God. In an effort to avoid fear and insecurity, we prefer doing everything ourselves.

Until fairly recently, I not only assumed independence was the mark of maturity, but viewed neediness as a character flaw. I dismissed verses such as "Let the little children come to me, and do not stop them; for it is to such as these that the kingdom of God belongs" (Luke 18:16 NRSV) and instead favored ones that exhort us to grow up and wean from our mother's breast (Heb. 5:11–14). It's embarrassing to admit, but I actually believed that self-sufficiency made me better than those needy people. Apparently, I'm not the only one who holds this warped logic.

A friend recounted the story of going to speak in a church where he knew no one. This man, a prominent leader and author, always worships with physical abandon. As the band played their last note, he walked from the sanctuary floor toward the podium, only to be stopped by the senior pastor, who asked, "Where do you think you're going?" He introduced himself and said, "I'm your speaker." The pastor breathed a sigh of relief and added, "Oh good. I thought you were one of those needy people." Without missing a beat, my friend candidly assured him, "I am one of those needy people—and I'm also your speaker this morning."[3]

Neediness offends us. We prefer not to depend on others because they might fail us, think poorly of us, or cause us to lose the respect and affirmation we so desperately want. Autonomy reinforces our self-perception of competence and strength. Conversely, depending on God and others confronts us with the reality that we are weak and can neither fulfill our marriage vows nor satisfy the command to love, apart from ongoing assistance and divine intervention. If we discount our need for God's daily bread or ignore our perseverant self-deception, our faith becomes corrupted with pride and self-importance—what the Greeks called hubris.

Scripture corrects this heretical mind-set. According to the prophet Isaiah, "We all, like sheep, have gone astray, each of us has turned to our own way" (Isa. 53:6 NIV). The apostle Paul writes, "All have sinned and fall short of the glory of God" (Rom. 3:23 NIV). No matter how deeply it offends us, we must confront our inherent waywardness as well as our impotence to reach God apart from Jesus.

We might be fooled into thinking that we need Christ only when we're in the midst of a crisis. The truth is, any patience, kindness, or love I show to Christopher originates from God, not me. And even if I could take credit for these traits, none of them bridges the gap between me and the Almighty or helps me become the kind of wife that I truly long to be. If I want to be more Christlike and love my husband well, I have to push off from the myth of self-sufficiency, bow my knee to Jesus, and ask for help. Repeatedly. It doesn't matter if you struggle with the same besetting sins that I do. All of us need transformation and all of us need Jesus in order to be transformed.

What Does Transformation Look Like?

It's not always obvious to us why we need to change. Mike Mason explains:

> Marriage, even under the very best of circumstances, is a crisis—one of the major crises of life—and it is a dangerous thing not to be aware of this. Whether it turns out to be a healthy, challenging, and constructive crisis, or a disastrous nightmare, depends largely upon how willing the partners are to be changed, how malleable they are.[4]

I was largely unaware of the malleability factor until we were married for several years. In my teens and twenties, I had deeply embedded control issues. (In other words, I was definitely not malleable.) What enabled me to function with some degree of competence was living like an emotional agnostic. I pretended that nothing affected me. I shut down the anger and turned off the tears. And then at age thirty-three, I became a mother. The energy that I previously directed toward holding it all together and propping up my mask was redirected to more primal activities, such as preventing our three sons from destroying the house or impaling one another with their homemade weapons. I felt like a character on a televised reality show, constantly exposing my imperfections to the world. Pretending to be perfect and hiding my weaknesses no longer worked. It was time to change.

In the book of Ezekiel, God promises the Israelites, "I will give you a new heart and put a new spirit in you; I will remove from you your heart of stone and give you a heart of flesh" (36:26 NIV). When I decided to make that initial step toward Jesus thirty-five years ago, God pried open my chest cavity to begin extricating the rock. During certain seasons, the process of change has felt messy, painful, and slow—sometimes so slow that I despaired. But then when I least expected it, God broke through.

Often these God-breathed breakthroughs profoundly improve our marriages. Perhaps after months of resistance, you finally feel able to forgive your spouse for lying to you. Or maybe you discover the grace to not simply overlook his most annoying habit but also love him even as he spreads his belongings over every flat surface, misplaces his car keys (again), or loudly slurps his morning beverage.

Such internal shifts remind us that God is at work and that real change is indeed possible. If in the process of change we consistently orient ourselves toward Him, our vertical relationship will empower us to love horizontally. We see the clearest example of how this happens "in the one person who lived his whole life closely and consistently in relation to God—Jesus."[5]

This movement toward Christ and holiness is meant to influence every component of our lives and of our marriages. As we become like Jesus, we willingly and continuously sacrifice for our spouses rather than protect our self-interests. We extend grace and mercy rather than judgment or retribution. We love lavishly rather than withhold in self-protection and fear. This kind of transformation will sometimes feel elusive and will always force us to confront the abject poverty of our souls. Paul poetically describes this mysterious process: "We all, who with unveiled faces contemplate the Lord's glory, are being transformed into his image with ever-increasing glory, which comes from the Lord, who is the Spirit" (2 Cor. 3:18 NIV).

As I let go of control, admit my brokenness, and allow others to see me, it feels more vulnerable than glorious. But it's also incredibly liberating. I now ask for help all the time. I no longer think of myself as better than those needy people because, like my speaker friend, I know I'm one of them. This process of becoming more emotionally alive as I mature spiritually has deepened our marriage. I know there are moments (perhaps seasons) when Christopher wishes I would regress and stop sharing my feelings, but in general he appreciates my transparency. This change frees him from having to guess what's going on in my head. His steadfast love and acceptance allow me to trust him more fully, which increases our emotional *and* sexual intimacy.

Such profound change does not happen magically or instantaneously. We have to want to grow, want to love more consistently, and want to regularly bless our spouses. Athletes don't become world-class by standing up and making a onetime commitment. They train. They dedicate their lives to reaching their goals. Likewise, we will not become awesome wives and husbands simply by speaking earnest vows before our family members and friends.

Pastor and author Timothy Keller concisely states in *The Meaning of Marriage*, "Nothing can mature character like marriage."[6] The depth of maturation largely depends upon the desire to grow and willingness to humbly submit to and rely upon God. After two and a half decades together, Christopher and I have changed. Profoundly. And in the process, we have forged a deep bond of trust and created an incredibly rich relationship. We're not special. We simply refused to settle for mediocrity and chose to believe that God had the goods to back up His promises.

Christopher and I believe that God wants all of us to experience loving, joyful, intimate marriages. As we say yes to Him, He will be our greatest advocate and our most dependable resource, providing whatever we need to do the work. Are you ready?

Going Deeper

1. Name several of the most satisfying, life-giving components of your marriage. How would you describe an ongoing frustration or struggle? As you read through *Making Marriage Beautiful*, ask God to help you grow in at least two specific areas.

2. Do you typically embrace or resist change? If the latter, do you know why? Think of a recent situation that necessitated change. How did that go? Is there anything you could have done differently?

3. How comfortable are you with the doctrine of sin? Can you easily identify your sins, even the less obvious ones?

4. Are you aware of how your sins and limitations affect your spouse? If not, ask your spouse. (But don't ask until you are able to listen without getting defensive or angry.)

5. Consider making this a daily prayer: "God, help me to see my spouse through Your eyes and love with Your heart."

2

NOT YOUR MOTHER'S LASAGNA

Legacies, Wounds, and Unrealistic Expectations

It's November and Christopher and I have made it through the first six months of marriage. So far so good. The many storms predicted by our well-meaning friends have blown north of us. We successfully dodge the "Where do we spend our first holiday?" conflict with the flip of a coin. It's heads, so we decide to drive five hours west to his home in central New York and disappoint my parents this year.

From a sociologist's perspective, our two families of origin are more similar than not. We both hail from white, working-class communities, our fathers went off to the Korean War, our mothers mostly stayed at home, and we each have two siblings. But if you peeled back the veneer, you would notice significant differences, especially if you happened to stop in during dinnertime.

In my northern European household, meals were civilized affairs. We sat at the kitchen table 357 nights a year. The dining room table was reserved for major holidays, birthdays, and 1,000-piece jigsaw puzzles. We never raised our voices or interrupted one another and always valued the quality of food over quantity. (Notice any moralizing in that sentence? We'll get to that momentarily.) In Christopher's Italian American home, life centered around one of five strategically placed tables. The question wasn't *if* you would sit at the table; it was which one. To this day, his parents' home has a table in the kitchen, dining room, basement, screened porch, and on the back deck. The table holds epic symbolism in the Greco household.

During our first Thanksgiving together, as soon as we claimed a spot at the table (the one in the dining room), I began to realize just how different our families were. There was twice as much food as we needed, including lime Jell-O and canned green beans submerged in a thick gray sauce. The turkey was ceremoniously placed front and center, and then his mother brought out two huge trays of lasagna. Lasagna. With extra sauce and meatballs. For Thanksgiving.

After a prayer, the curtain went up and the opera began. Unlike at my home, there was no turn taking or insightful follow-up questions. One person simply started talking—to no one in particular—and then another layered their thoughts on top but not before turning up the volume. Then a third and fourth jumped in, making it impossible to really listen to anyone—something I eventually learned was not a priority. I've never been a fan of opera and even less so when I'm thrust into it without an opportunity to rehearse my lines. This experience helped me better understand

Christopher, but I was not able to extrapolate his genetically coded mealtime expectations until we had a substantial fight not long after.

At our inaugural dinner party, we invited three couples over. Unlike Christopher's family of origin, we had only one table, which was woefully inadequate for eight adults. We made do. The conversation was lively and the food excellent. Everyone seemed to enjoy the evening—except Christopher, who made several less-than-affirming comments about my culinary efforts.

This same scenario played out multiple times before I pointedly inquired, "Why are you so critical of how I prepare meals for guests?" He shot back, "Because you don't cook enough food and you never put out extra sauce when you make pasta!" Want to guess how our evening played out? That fight opened our eyes to a shocking reality: our family cultures had so deeply shaped our preferences, biases, and beliefs that we each reflexively judged anything different as wrong. This discovery allowed us to start tracing other marital challenges directly back to our formative years.

By normalizing our own family's quirks and customs and concluding that our version of reality was morally superior, we had become ethnocentric. This term describes a tendency to assume the inherent superiority of one's own culture or ethnicity. I was guilty of ethnocentrism when I harshly evaluated his family's Thanksgiving traditions. He was guilty of ethnocentrism when he judged me as incompetent simply because I didn't put extra marinara sauce on the table.

Like us, many of you may have ended up with overweight luggage as you packed for your honeymoon because you unknowingly crammed the suitcase full of culturally bound expectations and historic wounds. If we lack awareness regarding our ethnocentrism and our scars, we tend to become oppositional and needlessly criticize and judge one another. Chapters 2 through 4 will help you identify your wounds, expectations, and preferences and free you to accept and enjoy your spouse's otherness.

In the Beginning: How Our Families Form Us

We don't emerge from the womb with fully formed personalities. Some of our likes and dislikes, strengths and weaknesses are genetic (nature), while others are learned (nurture). The moment we draw in our first breath, we begin absorbing information that incrementally shapes us. Along the way, we might remember those important milestones often recorded for posterity: first bike ride, first day of kindergarten, first communion. But it's often the more mundane experiences—most of which we can't recall and have no photographic record of—that actually shape us.

Our families of origin play powerful roles in our development. Parents and siblings teach us interpersonal skills, such as how to communicate, what emotions are acceptable, how to navigate (or avoid) conflicts, and how to accept (or reject) those who are different from us. This happens whether our family is Kenyan, Colombian, or Korean, though the specific ethnicity unequivocally informs the process.

Much of this identity building happens before our language develops, and that's part of why it's difficult for us to have specific memories. For instance, approximately forty-eight hours after entering the world, a newborn's eyes are able to focus eight to ten inches, which happens to be the distance from the mother's breast to the mother's eyes.[1] Studies have shown that newborns constantly scan their mother's face, searching for love, reassurance, and acceptance.[2] Similarly, as infants, we listened to our mother's tone of voice and learned how our behavior affected her.

These are not random snippets of developmental psychology. We continue to feel the repercussions of our parents' caregiving long after we've moved out. During Christopher's teenage years, his mother openly vocalized her disappointment about him and his siblings. Lacking other options, Christopher defended himself against her but also unknowingly internalized her criticisms. To this day, when I express any frustration with him, even over minor issues, my voice resonates with the memory of his mother, triggering defensiveness and shame.

Thankfully, for many of us, the positive influences outweigh the negative. Two of the greatest legacies my parents imparted were the gift of hospitality and a love for travel. Growing up, we constantly had people in our home, from exchange students to touring West Point cadets to distant relatives. One summer afternoon, an out-of-state van crashed up the street. Without hesitation, my mother invited these strangers over for dinner while their father went to the emergency room for treatment. Her willingness to extend herself and share our limited resources influenced my understanding of what it means to offer hospitality. It doesn't surprise me that since getting married, Christopher and I have had approximately twenty international and graduate students live with us.

My family valued our annual vacation just as deeply as we valued hospitality. When we were young, we spent a week every summer at a turquoise-blue motel overlooking the Atlantic Ocean. Later we crisscrossed the United States, occasionally towing a pop-up camper behind us. By the time I was thirty, I had visited forty-five states, Mexico, the Caribbean, and Europe. Vacations were sacrosanct, and I eagerly anticipated how Christopher and I would continue this tradition. Unfortunately, his family followed a different manual. They took only one travel vacation during his entire childhood, in part because they valued spending time with their local extended family. It was only five years ago that Christopher and I were finally able to plan and navigate an entire vacation without major conflict. Now it's one of our favorite things to do together. That's growth.

It may be surprising to discover how many of our present-day likes and dislikes have been influenced by our families of origin. For the most part, we move through life largely unaware of the preferences we're stockpiling and how they influence our marriages. But make no mistake: we do stockpile and they do influence us. There's one more specific element that shapes the expectations we carry for our spouses: our emotional wounds.

Recognizing Scar Tissue: Family-Related Wounds

Obviously, there are far more consequential takeaways from our childhood years than where we went for vacation or what we ate for Thanksgiving dinner. Despite the reality that our mothers and fathers longed to parent well, none of them did it perfectly. Some of us have ugly, jagged scars as a result of our parents' abuse, abandonment, or neglect. Others of us have more discreet wounds from being undervalued, dismissed, or misunderstood. My wounds are of the latter variety.

As far back as I can remember, I have been a highly sensitive person. One of my earliest memories is playing in the sandbox and repeatedly asking my mother to take off my little blue sneakers and dump out the sand. While I can now tolerate sand touching my bare skin, I've not outgrown my sensitivities: I continue to cut scratchy tags off my shirts, sleep with blackout shades, and request that restaurant managers turn down the background music. My parents were good people, but they didn't seem to understand my profound sensitivities. Cue painful memory.

Our family's Sunday evening ritual included a humble dinner of tomato soup with grilled cheese sandwiches followed by two hours of television. One particular night, *Mutual of Omaha's Wild Kingdom* aired an episode on seal hunting in Greenland. Heartless men clubbed these beautiful animals, creating crimson pools of blood on the pristine snow. Everything about this horrified me, and I burst into tears. Rather than comforting me or offering to change the channel, my parents laughed. A not-so-sensitive child would have shrugged this off and forgotten about it. Not me. I fled to the safety of my room, slamming the door behind me. That was the last time I cried in front of my parents. Lesson learned? Emotional honesty is dangerous. Withholding or denying emotions is safer. Though denying my emotions spared me from being misunderstood or rejected, it also caused me to mistrust others and feel invisible.

Without much effort, most of us can recall single incidents or recurring childhood patterns that continue to replay in our lives against our wishes. When Christopher was in middle school, the Air Force transferred his father from upstate New York to Missouri. His dad spent that first year alone while the rest of the family waited it out, hoping that he would receive a transfer back east. That transfer never materialized, so they all moved to Kansas City. Christopher went from having an enormous family network (his mom was one of eight children) and solid friendships to being an outsider and on the receiving end of much bullying. He's smart. He quickly figured out that if he recited television and movie dialogues—particularly from Monty Python—his peers would laugh and find another target. Lesson learned? Boys are dangerous and words are powerful.

Given these two stories, is it any wonder that whenever tension surfaced between us, I would shut down and Christopher would embark on endless monologues? Thankfully, he steered clear of British humor.

Race-Related Wounds

Because Christopher and I are white, we have not been victims of racial discrimination. However, many of you not only have been but continue to be affected by this systemic sin. The highly publicized race-related issues of recent times have shattered any illusion that racism is a thing of the past. If you are a minority, you have most likely been traumatized by racial disparity, intentional segregation, and overt discrimination. It's nearly impossible to grow up with an intact sense of self if you have been repeatedly told that you are less than and flawed. These deep wounds guide not only how we understand ourselves but also how we interact with others.

Evan, a Chinese American friend, grew up in a predominantly white neighborhood during the seventies. He doesn't look back on his neighbors as racists but rather ignorant and ethnocentric. In his words:

> My personality was reduced to my ethnic identity. There was a sense that everything that represented my family of origin was not accepted in the culture. I had to put on different masks and code-switch [modifying the way you express yourself depending on who you're with]. I remember as young as first grade, maybe earlier, looking in the mirror and wishing that my facial features were different because I didn't look like everyone else. In Chinese culture, it's considered beautiful to have a wide, flat nose, but in American culture, it's beautiful if you have a long, thin nose. I would sit in front of the mirror and squeeze my nose, hoping that it would become long and narrow. Think about how powerful the messages must have been for me as a seven-year-old child to feel that I had to change my face to be accepted.

Regardless of how we got our scars and how they manifest, they don't magically disappear when we get married. We bring all of who we are into our marital covenants: our gifts, talents, and strengths but also our weaknesses, limitations, and brokenness.

Our spouses are typically the first people who have gotten close enough to notice these scars.

How Preferences and Scars Morph into Expectations

These wounds, personal preferences, and internalized cultural values not only inform our beliefs and actions but also become the foundation for many of our expectations. As we enter into marriage, we have dozens of unspoken expectations for the small, seemingly incidental details of life together (e.g., who cleans the bathroom?) as well as the major, significant components of life (e.g., who sacrifices their career to care for a sick child or aging parent?). Sometimes we're not even cognizant of our expectations until others fail to meet them. Sometimes an expectation emanates out of our wounds, which makes it more difficult for us to identify the expectation, let alone discern what drives it.

For example, not long after we were married, Christopher and I started having conflicts about what it meant to be home in time for dinner. After we negotiated what seemed like a reasonable compromise and then he showed up an hour (or more) late, I felt angry. He would apologize, but then we'd have a déjà vu moment the following week. Though I had legitimate reasons to be frustrated, his offense was a level three (out of ten—not that big a deal) and my response was a level eight (in other words, out of proportion). This disparity clued me in to the possibility that *maybe* this dynamic was uncovering a historic wound.

When we have the same conflicts over and over again, it's likely that there's something deeper going on that will provide an opportunity for healing if we can stop reacting and start exploring what's driving our broken patterns. That was certainly true regarding our ongoing discord about mealtime. When I was twelve, my grandfather died and our extended family fractured due to some poor choices and miscommunication. After two of my father's beloved siblings moved out of state, he turned to liquor to numb his pain. This eventually led to a full-blown alcohol addiction lasting more than a decade.

During my middle and high school years, dinner could be a tense affair. *Would Dad be on time? Would he be sober? If he wasn't, how would Mom respond?* There was an obvious connection between my childhood wounds and our marital strife. Christopher's struggle with time management uncovered my unresolved pain and amplified my unprocessed anger. My response replicated my family of origin's patterns and certainly did not help Christopher feel loved or grow in his time management skills.

Obviously, not all expectations emerge from brokenness and pain. Many are inspired by God. When we vow to love, honor, and cherish until death do us part, we expect our spouses to stick with us, even if we become unemployed, cannot conceive, or develop serious health issues. We expect our spouses to tell the truth, advocate for us, and remain monogamous. These are healthy nonnegotiables. We should all discern which expectations are godly and life-giving and which ones adversely affect our marriages. This is exactly what my friends Evan and Samantha have done so well.

Evan and Samantha's Story

Evan, whom I introduced a few pages back, and his wife, Samantha, increase the emotional intelligence of any gathering. They bring their vast creativity and warmth into parenting, work, and leadership. As an interracial couple, their journey to understand their hidden expectations and historic wounds has been slightly more complex. Evan started the interview by talking about how being a minority has affected him.

> **Evan:** Growing up, I felt there was no embracing multiculturalism. You had to assimilate. It was an indirect and direct message about feeling less than, even in simple experiences. I remember that one day as my grandmother walked me to the bus stop, she was talking to me in Chinese and all the kids started making fun of her. As a young kid, you internalize all of these instances to know that you are different and then downplay the differences to fit in.
>
> When Sam and I got married, this mentality continued. One of the ways I worked to fit in was through bearing the burden of changing when tension surfaced between us. Early on, there were expectations that there was one particular way of living, and I always seemed to be wrong. Because

of my people-pleasing nature, I conformed to Sam's wishes. It got to the point that I was conforming so much that I was losing my identity. I broke down because I felt that I didn't know who I was anymore. Even though I had a sense of the cultural differences, I didn't know how to talk about them. I didn't have the language. Because Samantha thought that her way was right, I feared I'd have to go through the rest of my life feeling that I was wrong.

Samantha: I had no idea I was doing this. No clue. I was telling him how I felt. I was saying, "These are things you could do as a spouse." In the meantime, I was diminishing him. Evan would say, "I can't do that." Because all the marriage books were telling me that I needed to communicate my needs, I assumed I was doing everything by the book.

We ultimately went to a marriage counselor who suggested that our cultural differences were causing most of our issues. Not long afterward, I realized that those marriage books contributed to the problem because they were all authored by Caucasian, Western writers.

Such books will be effective if the couple is from the same culture and the same rules apply to both parties, but no book we found addressed what it's like to be married to someone from another culture, where the underlying and unwritten rules are totally different.

When I was making "I" statements, I was going by the Western marriage books, but I had no clue I was breaking all of his ingrained cultural rules. In Asian culture, you don't start with "I" at all. You start with "we." According to this set of values, I give him the benefit of the doubt up front, let him save face, and might even take the blame upon myself or at least look at how I could change. If he does the same with me, we move from a place of discord to a place of harmony—another Asian value. This is very different than my culture of owning my stuff and asking him to do the same.

Since then, Evan and Samantha have been faithfully working to understand how their embedded expectations impinge upon their marriage, including everything from time management to spending habits.

Samantha: Our ethnic values on money completely clashed. I have more of a Protestant, Yankee background. You don't spend money; you save it. It's a moral value to be frugal. Evan believes in frugality, but we have different spending habits.

Evan: I would go to Costco and buy all this stuff, and then Samantha would give it away because it was stressful for her to have it around. My parents grew up during the war, so there was a scarcity mentality. The idea of abundance was comforting. I valued getting the most for our money.

Samantha: I did not share this value. I hate warehouse shopping. We don't need to shop for twelve people! When he would come home from Costco with huge bags of supplies, I would instantly feel overwhelmed.

Evan: Over time, we figured out how our family-of-origin expectations were influencing our buying habits and discovered the unifying value of simplicity, which has since shaped our spending.

Samantha: It's taken years for me to reprogram myself. I've cried so much about all of this. I come from a very ethnocentric family. Having other cultures around me, learning how they grew up, and gaining another perspective have helped. There's a lot of internal work that the Holy Spirit has done in me. I see Evan with much more compassion now, and I choose to believe the best about him. I no longer view him as the opponent.

Evan: God is showing me how to love Samantha and her culture. We now talk about our conflicts in ways that are honoring and affirming instead of moralizing and criticizing. When you first get married, it's really important to be right. As you get older, you realize that it's not about being right; it's about being sure that the relationship is right.

Because Evan and Samantha learned how their historic wounds and cultural preferences influenced their expectations, they were able to step back from any entrenched positions and increasingly find common ground. By choosing the path of humility and depending on God to lead them, their hearts have changed and their marriage has been transformed.

Though the path Christopher and I have taken is not exactly the same as Evan and Samantha's, we too have learned the importance of valuing each other's opinions and realigning our expectations. As we have pursued healing for our historic wounds, repented of our moralizing, and committed to honoring each other's traditions, we're less dogmatic and more flexible. These changes manifest in small but welcome ways. When I need to talk through something, Christopher no longer expects me to replicate his family's operatic style of communication. And when we have company, I try to serve more food than I know we need because I want to validate rather than dismiss his traditions. Sometimes, I even remember to put extra sauce on the table.

Going Deeper

1. Did your unique personality and gifts receive affirmation or criticism within your family? How does your family's response continue to affect you?

2. Describe the blessings of growing up in your family, specifically the ones related to your cultural heritage. Now describe the challenges. How do the blessings and challenges currently affect your marriage?

3. Did you experience any sexism, racism, or other "isms" during your childhood? If so, did they result in any core lies that continue to influence you or your marriage? If so, how?

4. Are there specific expectations that you hold that your spouse has been unable to fulfill? List them and then prayerfully explore how these expectations and any ensuing disappointments might be hurting your marriage. Which ones are godly and good, and which ones might you be better off letting go?

5. How important is it for you to be right rather than make sure the relationship is right? Ask your spouse if he or she agrees with your assessment.

3

BEYOND PINK
AND BLUE

Creating Christ–Centered Gender Expectations

Christopher and I sometimes refuse to comply with the gender stereotypes presented to us by American culture. For example, one evening a few years back, Christopher practiced the piano while I installed our new dishwasher. He didn't offer to help, and I didn't ask. He deeply appreciates my willingness to take on home-improvement projects and feels no compulsion to rescue me or take over. Frankly, he's relieved. His personal strategy regarding repairs tends to be "If I can't fix it with duct tape or hot glue, I'll overlook it." When similar situations played out earlier in our marriage, I tended to resent him. This time, I enjoyed being serenaded. We were making progress.

We chose not to conform to traditional gender norms long before we got married. I played competitive sports from kinder-garten through college and then worked in the male-dominated field of news and sports photography for nearly two decades. During high school, Christopher opted for chorus and theater. To this day, he feels more at ease on a stage with a microphone than on a court with any type of spherical object. In fact, after years of basketball games with our sons, his layups still resemble Fred Astaire with a charley horse. However, he slam-dunks me in the emotional-relational realm. Not only can he skillfully lead a roomful of people in a fruitful discussion, but he also knows what he's feeling at every given moment and willingly shares those feelings with me.

If you imagine that we've always appreciated and respected these profound and quirky differences, you would be wrong. Until fairly recently, we toggled between shame, disappointment, and anger. Why have we struggled to appreciate each other's uniqueness? Primarily because we're sinful but also because of the extrabiblical gender expectations we unwittingly carried into our marriage.

Even if you fit more neatly into traditional gender roles than Christopher and I do, you probably also brought a few gender-based expectations into your marriage that occasionally result in conflict and hurt feelings—or worse. The fact that some church cultures have unwritten rules for men's and women's behavior further complicates this matter.

For years, Christopher and I struggled to discern what caused several of our recurring battles. Through much trial and error, we learned to unpack our conflicts by asking, *Where did these specific expectations come from? Does the Bible validate these expectations?* And perhaps most important, *Do these expectations help or hinder us from honoring each other?* We will explore these and other questions throughout this chapter.

I'm well aware that conversations about gender have the potential to arouse suspicion and polarize us, perhaps more so within faith communities. If the preceding paragraphs raise red flags, let me clarify. I believe that men and women are purposefully created with distinct gender differences that should not be ignored or downplayed. I also believe the arc of Scripture promotes marriage as a covenant between one man and one woman for life. Furthermore, I am not advocating gender neutrality or gender fluidity. I am advocating that we examine our gender-based expectations through the lens of Scripture—rather than secular or church culture—to the end goal of helping each other flourish.

Christopher and I have found that it's rarely fruitful to conform—or try to make each other conform—to rigid, binary gender roles, particularly if we have not prayerfully and thoroughly discussed the implications of these roles. Whether we're considering mundane household responsibilities or more consequential roles, God offers us a wide variety of options regarding how we live out our calling in the context of marriage. As we learn to identify any extrabiblical gender expectations that we impose on each other and then choose to release our spouses from those expectations, we can esteem, enjoy, and appreciate the actual person we married rather than try to make them conform to our preconceived expectations.

Why Gender Matters

At the pinnacle of creation,

> God said, "Let us make human beings in our
> image, to be like us...."
>> So God created human beings in his own
>>> image.
>>> In the image of God he created them;
>>> male and female he created them.
>>>> (Gen. 1:26–27)

Several remarkable concepts are found in this short passage. First, unlike all other creatures, God created us in His image so that we would reveal and represent Him on the face of the earth. We often fail to appreciate the wonder and staggering implications of this reality.

Second, an individual man or woman cannot fully reflect God. Author and theologian Carolyn Custis James explains, "Adam is one. But the God he represents is plural—a Trinitarian *three in one*. A solitary image bearer cannot adequately or accurately reveal God in the world, much less fulfill his destiny as a human being."[1] Because the Trinity consists of both masculine and feminine attributes, men and women image the triune God more fully when they create and participate in collaborative partnerships (marriage or otherwise).

If we fail to live according to God's template as equal but different creations, we may unwittingly reject our unique callings and devalue His intentional design. This can leave us edging toward polar opposites: gender rigidity on one extreme (locking ourselves into specific, socially accepted roles) or gender elasticity on the other (pushing beyond the healthy boundaries of one's given gender, or refusing to accept one's masculinity or femininity).[2] How, then, can we find a middle ground that allows us to live securely in our own gender and faithfully represent the One who made us? Perhaps first we need to discern exactly what gender is and why it matters.

Gender is deeply connected to one's sex, which is determined in utero, and is fixed for life. Author Debra Hirsch writes, "The term *sex* (as a category) is now generally used to refer to a person's *biological sex* (i.e., male or female)."[3] By contrast, author Mark Yarhouse says,

> Gender refers to the psychological, social and cultural aspects of being male or female.... Gender identity is often associated with gender role. Gender role, then, refers to ways in which people adopt cultural expectations for maleness or femaleness. This includes but is not limited to academic interests, career pursuits and so on.[4]

We cannot divorce ourselves from our sex or our gender without some level of personal disintegration and without partially concealing the *imago Dei* within us. Because our bodies were designed by God, *in His image*, they reveal God's kingdom and aspects of His character. For instance, the Hebrew word *tsela* (typically translated as "rib" in Genesis 2:21–22) often means one side of a sacred architectural structure such as the temple.[5] This seems to imply that male and female bodies are purposefully designed not only to fit together but also to hint at something greater, just as historic temples and cathedrals were created to reference God through their design (e.g., in the shape of a cross).

Furthermore, we all have specific attributes connected to our anatomy and physiology, such as nurture and strength, that reference God's nature. It seems that "something about us reveals something about our Creator."[6] A woman's ability to grow an infant inside her womb powerfully displays nurture, which is one component of God's character. I don't believe that only women can nurture nor am I insinuating that God is a giant womb, but we can't dismiss scriptures such as Isaiah 42:14, where God says, "Like a woman in labor, I will cry and groan and pant"; Matthew 23:37, where Jesus refers to Himself as "a hen gather[ing] her chicks under her wings" (NIV); or the verses in the gospel of John that refer to the Holy Spirit as the Comforter (John 14:16, 26; 15:26; 16:7 KJV). Clearly, the triune God—Father, Son, and Holy Spirit—nurtures, or tenderly cares for, His people.

Along with nurture, strength is unequivocally one of God's character traits: "Ascribe to the LORD, O heavenly beings, ascribe to the LORD glory and strength" (Ps. 29:1 NRSV). Just as a womb is not a prerequisite for nurturing, a Y chromosome is not a prerequisite for exhibiting strength. Nurture and strength—as well as many other attributes—are part of God's nature. "[God] can be recognized in the strong characteristics of both male and female image-bearers, because he transcends the categories we understand."[7] Therefore, when we nurture others, exhibit strength, or walk in any other godly attributes, we reference God.

God always creates with intentionality. He could have made us asexual—capable of reproducing by budding or division, as happens with many plants and some invertebrates—but He chose not to. Our by-design differentness allows us to procreate in a wildly pleasurable fashion while we simultaneously complement and fulfill one another. Perhaps this is why when Adam first saw Eve, he joyfully declared, "At last! ... This one is bone from my bone, and flesh from my flesh!" (Gen. 2:23). He was essentially saying, *Now I have someone who is like me but not me. And when I am with her, I am more completely myself.*

How Has the Gift Become a Curse?

If this otherness is both intentional and deeply meaningful, why does it cause so much trouble? At least in part, the trouble started in the Garden of Eden when our ancestors assumed they knew better than God.

Between the creation and the fall, Adam and Eve lived in complete harmony. There was no nagging, exasperated sighing, eye rolling, or dismissive reactivity that so many of us have come to expect when we engage with the other gender. We can assume their perfect relationship with God the Father empowered them to love and respect each other all day, every day. Enviable, isn't it?

But when the Enemy sidled up to the two of them and intimated that perhaps God was not trustworthy (Gen. 3:1–6), their harmony turned to discord. After they disobeyed, they no longer stood side by side as a unified front. Instead, fear and shame compelled them to cower, hide from God, and turn against each other.

God then described how their rebellion would play out, not just in their lifetime but in all generations to come:

> Then he said to the woman,
>> "I will sharpen the pain of your pregnancy,
>>> and in pain you will give birth.
>> And you will desire to control your husband
>>> but he will rule over you."
> And to the man he said,
>> "Since you listened to your wife and ate
>>> from the tree
>> whose fruit I commanded you not
>>> to eat,
>> the ground is cursed because of you.
>>> All your life you will struggle to scratch
>>> a living from it." (Gen. 3:16–17)

Since then, our relational and vocational callings have been affected by sin's legacy. Rather than living and laboring as equals who are subordinate only to God, we often create gender hierarchies that culminate in idolatrous relationships.[8] Instead of appreciating and honoring our intentional differences, we tend to disrespect and devalue each other. Furthermore, sin somehow uniquely targets each gender. Many men have to fight against the impulse to dominate and exploit. If they succumb to that broken inclination, they corrupt their relationships with one another, with women, and with the earth. Women have to fight against the impulse to judge men as incompetent and untrustworthy. If we give in, we end up trying to control men rather than trust and respect them.

We don't need the latest issue of *People* magazine to see how sin distorts male-female relationships—it's evident in Scripture: Abraham slept with his slave Hagar; King David abused his power and took advantage of Bathsheba; Gomer was unfaithful to Hosea; and Delilah manipulated and betrayed Samson.

Though my hard-heartedness has never been quite as dramatic as these Old Testament examples, there have been seasons when I have failed to appreciate Christopher's otherness. Years ago, we brought home bedbugs after a brief hotel stay. The moment we discovered this nightmare, I was near hysterics. Christopher remained calm and began analyzing the top bedbug-sniffing beagles in the region. I didn't want Greco analytics; I wanted a hug and reassurance that my feelings were valid despite the mucus cascading from my nostrils. Apparently, in certain situations, Christopher and I totally conform to gender stereotypes.

Pastor Timothy Keller succinctly describes the inherent tension of otherness:

> Inside a real marriage there will be conflicts rooted in gender differences that are seismic. It is not simply that the other gender is different; it's that his or her differences *make no sense*. And once we come up against this wall of incomprehensibility, the sin in our heart tends to respond by assigning moral significance to what is simply a deep temperamental difference.[9]

Our differentness creates tension and conflict because, quite honestly, we want the other not to be so other—we prefer that they be more like us. If we want to truly love and honor our spouses, we must learn to accept and celebrate their otherness. By simply bookmarking it with bland indifference, we potentially disrespect our creator God and our spouses. Furthermore, we also miss out on the many ways God intends to reveal Himself and bless us through those who are different. Before we can experience the blessing of otherness, we may need to discern the origin of our gender expectations.

Where Do Our Expectations Come From?

At least four sources influence our expectations regarding gender and gender roles: family, culture, subculture (church community, ethnic community, and so on), and Scripture. I want to briefly explore the role of family and the culture at large in this process.

First, family. From age two through adulthood, we're constantly forming and revising expectations regarding gender identity and gender roles. As children and young adolescents, we watch and mimic, slowly figuring out who we want to be. During our second main period of individuation (the terrible twos being the first and the terrible teens being the second), we begin to establish our own beliefs and behavioral patterns largely influenced by what we witnessed during the first ten to twelve years of our lives.

Christopher and I have families that were equal parts the same and different. My father was a man of few words but many deeds. He could fix anything. His workbench looked like a Craftsman catalog, including every possible size hammer, screwdriver, and wrench. Though Christopher's father has some aptitude for repairs, he never liked doing them, and most endeavors were punctuated by exasperated swearing, always in Italian. Once, after Christopher helped his father put up paneling in the basement, his dad asked him what he'd learned. Christopher wryly responded, "I learned that when I grow up, I'm going to hire people to do this" (or, as Providence would have it, rely upon said father-in-law). It's impossible to dismiss how these formative experiences with an angry father shaped his aversion to home repairs.

My sisters and I learned how to use the washing machine at an early age and were expected to take care of our own clothes. Because Christopher's mother enjoyed doing the laundry and was slightly territorial about this task, he didn't wash his clothes until he went away to college. Though laundry duty was not commingled with an angry parent, my enthusiasm for this task mirrors Christopher's feelings about doing home repairs.

When we got married, we were both guilty of magical thinking. I assumed Christopher would gradually become interested in fixing things and we'd never have to hire a repairperson. He assumed I would wash and iron his dress shirts and then place them on evenly spaced, wooden hangers. I can assure you, I have plumbers, electricians, and carpenters on speed dial, and if Christopher wants his clothes ironed, he's on his own. It's now humorous to me that neither of us understood how deeply our parents' strengths and weaknesses influenced our expectations of each other. But they did. (And *humorous* is not the word that we would use to describe our early conflicts over these issues.)

Culture shapes our expectations almost as profoundly as our families. Men and women in every culture across the globe internalize and conform to certain gender norms. Here in the United States, men are expected to amass power, exhibit strength, withhold emotion (except excitement at sporting events), enjoy using power tools, and idolize their careers. Women are supposed to supernaturally sequester all fat cells in our mammary glands, look perpetually thirty-two, control our emotions just enough so that men won't feel uncomfortable, love to shop, and idolize relationships. Some expectations seem to be universal, but not all are. In many Latin countries, emotionally distant men would be anomalies. In some African and Pacific Island nations, thin women are seen as unhealthy and less desirable as mates.

What Happens When We Fail to Live Up to Our Spouses' Expectations?

On a practical level, cultural expectations often result in a herd mentality that encourages conformity over individuation. Ever been at a social gathering where the women congregate in the kitchen prepping the food while the men talk about sports in a different room? Although such a reductionist tableau might be less common today than twenty years ago, it still happens. Gender roles help cultures function in a predictable, orderly fashion and for the most part are not inherently bad.

However, if our temperaments and natural abilities do not fall neatly into the prescribed cultural norms and if the gender hierarchies and roles are not firmly based in kingdom theology, they may constrain and diminish us. Though we might not be able to articulate what's happening, we may feel confused, angry, underappreciated, or even ashamed. If we don't want to deal with these raw emotions, we find it simpler to comply with what's expected. Would a man who preferred cooking to watching sports feel comfortable joining the women in the kitchen at the aforementioned gathering, or would he remain with the men and pretend to care who won the British Open that afternoon? Christopher chimes in, "The latter. Totally."

Most of us can handle temporarily conforming at a dinner party, but what happens over the long haul when our strengths and gifts are not valued by our spouses? What happens to our self-esteem and confidence when we perpetually fail to meet our spouses' expectations? It's the opposite of heaven coming down to earth. There's strife, self-hatred, shame, misogyny (hatred of women and of the feminine), and misandry (hatred of men and of the masculine).

Part of the reason Christopher does not enjoy home repairs is that he measures himself against the typical American male and finds himself lacking. In our culture, men are supposed to relish the challenge of fixing things. Because Christopher feels competent when he writes a worship song and incompetent when he tries to install a new appliance, he'll opt for the keyboard rather than the wrench if given the choice. Of course, it's not always possible to avoid our shame triggers.

Throughout his adult life, Christopher has experienced what he has come to know as shame attacks. He explains,

Regardless of the trigger—an interpersonal slight, an unexpected professional disappointment, or a broken sliding door I don't know how to fix—I feel energy go out of my body, and my head starts spinning with negative thoughts and worst-case scenarios. These shame attacks happen like the flip of a switch, and early on in our marriage, no amount of encouragement from Dorothy seemed able to stop me. I couldn't predict when the attack would strike or, unfortunately, how quickly I would be able to realize that it was happening, push back against it, and prevail. I now recognize that my shame is deeply rooted in a childish conviction that I am relegated to be a lower species than other men who are more overtly masculine. These feelings of victimization are irrational, and when I'm clearheaded, I know that these beliefs are false and sown by the Enemy.

Shame is one of the most pernicious consequences of unhealthy and ungodly gender expectations. Researcher Brené Brown defines shame as "the intensely painful feeling or experience of believing we are flawed and therefore unworthy of acceptance and belonging."[10] It affects men and women equally. For instance, women are supposed to enjoy talking on the phone. I love talking face-to-face but dislike talking on the phone. All my friends and family members know that if they call me, they will have to suffer through awkward pauses. Because I depart from this and other gender norms, I have to constantly resist the destructive forces of shame.

Shame not only turns inward but also tends to morph into anger or hatred and spills onto others. Misogyny and misandry are outward expressions of the enmity that has existed between men and women since the fall. Misogyny and misandry find expression in micro-aggressions, such as subtle comments about how emotionally incompetent men are, as well as macro-aggressions, such as domestic abuse or rape. The initial conflict in humanity was between the genders. Eve acted independently and did not consult Adam. Adam blamed Eve rather than accept responsibility. This pattern influences the relational DNA for all of us.

The impact of misogyny and misandry infiltrates our thinking and subsequently our actions. When we create biased conclusions about what our spouses can or can't, should or shouldn't do, we unfairly diminish them. If the wife is gifted in accounting and money management, the household will be well served if she does the family budget and pays the bills. If the husband is more adept with a chef's knife than a putty knife, the entire family will miss out if he is banished to the basement workbench.

Biology is often a determining factor for the gender roles and expectations we carry. A woman alone has the capacity to nurture life within her body and then provide physical sustenance after the baby is born. But if a mother has a career she loves and the father is eager to care for their young children, is there evidence that such a role reversal violates Scripture? Or does it simply deviate from our deeply embedded gender norms and make us feel uncomfortable?

According to Timothy Keller, "Rigid cultural gender roles have no Biblical warrant. Christians cannot make a scriptural case for masculine and feminine stereotypes."[11]

Again, I am by no means advocating gender neutrality or minimizing the beauty of motherhood. Just as with race, if we ignore our differences, we miss the gift of otherness. Instead, I am advocating that we explore any ambivalence with our God-given gifts and wrestle with the possibility that we are imposing extrabiblical, culturally bound expectations upon each other. We can discern this by paying attention to areas of conflict, routine disappointment, and unshakable shame; comparing our thoughts, expectations, and behaviors to Scripture (specifically how Jesus treated women and men); and prayerfully processing with our spouses. If we determine that we are holding on to unrealistic expectations for each other, we then have to begin the process of repenting and recalibrating.

Becoming Our True Gendered Selves in the Context of Marriage

We rarely turn to the book of Ruth for direction and insight on gender issues. Christianity's reading of this Old Testament account often reduces it to a traditional "man rescues damsel in distress" romance, but it's so much more. Ruth and Boaz refused to follow the cultural script for the gender norms of the day so that they could instead fulfill God's calling.

Within the first five verses, we learn that Naomi, Ruth's mother-in-law, had lost her husband and her two sons, one of whom was Ruth's husband. Once Naomi discovered that the famine in her homeland had lifted, she planned to return home and leave her two daughters-in-law in Moab. If Ruth had obeyed the rules of that time, she would have remained in Moab and remarried. Instead, she followed God's leading and returned to Bethlehem with Naomi. Not long after their arrival, Ruth again disregarded the limiting norms and approached Boaz's foreman, pleading for permission "to go where gleaners were not permitted, to work *among* the harvesters where plenty of newly cut grain lay waiting to be gathered into bundles."[12] Then, she pushed the boundaries to their limit by uncovering Boaz's feet as he slept, essentially proposing marriage to him.[13]

Because of her refusal to follow the script given to women in ancient culture, she saved her mother-in-law's life and became a root in Jesus's family tree (see Matt. 1:5). Similarly, Boaz also refused to be constrained by cultural definitions of manhood by investing his power "on behalf of those who have no power or voice in the community,"[14] risking his estate in the process.

And then there's Jesus. A close reading of Scripture communicates that the Messiah apparently never got the memo stating the rules and regulations about being a male leader. He did not take advantage of women but instead treated them with esteem and honor. When Mary poured nard on his feet (Luke 7:36–38), He defended her and her lavish display of love. As the disciples' king, He transcended hierarchal boundaries by washing their feet (John 13:1–17).

Yet Jesus was by no means solely a tender, gentle servant. He overturned the tables in the temple (Matt. 21:12), rebuked the leaders of His day, and endured a horrific death on the cross. Jesus clearly exhibited what we would consider to be masculine and feminine attributes and in so doing became "the prototype for what it means to be human."[15]

What implications does this have for our marriages? By pursuing Jesus rather than any distorted cultural standards, we can stop expending so much energy trying to fit in and instead respond to God's unique call. By adopting this framework, Christopher is free to stay home and pop in a DVD of a favorite Broadway play rather than watch the Super Bowl while downing beer with the guys. I can stop pretending I like shopping, a reality he increasingly appreciates.

This exploration of roles and expectations should not serve as an excuse to avoid certain tasks, particularly onerous ones. None of us need a revelation from God to take out the garbage, unclog toilets, or wash windows. Hopefully, we learn to consistently submit any areas where we lack gifting or desire and remain willing to grow, if not for our own sakes at least out of love for our spouses. (Just recently, Christopher did get down on his hands and knees to help me reinstall that same dishwasher after we had to temporarily disconnect it.)

Jon and Amy's Story

Jon and Amy are twentysomething professionals who have been married for seven years. They have thoughtfully discerned their gifts and aim to live authentically, even when their strengths don't line up with some of the typical Christian gender norms. I started by asking them about how they had individuated from some of the stereotypical gender roles.

> **Jon:** I've never wanted a woman who would take care of me—I've wanted a partner who had her own identity. My mom was a homemaker when I was growing up. When my siblings and I left, this gaping hole appeared. There was lots of pressure on my dad to provide for our family since she didn't work. All of this contributed to my feeling that when I get married, I don't want to have to earn all our money and I don't want my wife to feel that she is defined solely by raising children.

> **Amy:** Jon's perspective lifts a burden off me because many women who have careers still carry the responsibilities of the home too. Jon and I share everything equally. I love my home. I made the curtains. I throw a killer dinner party. I shouldn't be relegated to being a hard-nosed professional woman when I equally love my work *and* my home.
>
> That's not to say that our choices have always been understood. We are in no rush to have children, and I would say this is where we experience the most conflict. I definitely feel lonely because

I'm not traveling the same road as most other Christian women.

Jon: Because we've decided to wait to start a family, we get the occasional "When are you going to have kids?" line of questioning. No one has been cruel about it, but there is an expectation of a more traditional-looking route.

Another bump has been Amy's expectations. She wants a sensitive, gentle, caring man who is also traditionally driven and masculine. If I fall short of that list of requirements, which I do, then she's disappointed, which I don't like. Because my focus and drive to a career goal might be subtler or less driven than your average professional man, I've felt judgment from Amy. Of course the irony is that my temperament and career drive allow me to be more supportive and flexible, something that your average driven male executive would not be able or willing to pull off.

Amy: That's totally true. I want a powerful CEO husband, but I also want someone to clap for me and be my biggest fan. Double standard, right?

After assuring her that most of us are guilty of holding double standards, I asked them to describe the benefits of their unique choices.

Jon: It's been such a blessing to have a wife who is her own person. Because of our approach of being partners and doing life together as equals, we are able to do and accomplish a lot more. For instance, buying this house would not have happened if it were just the Jon show. We've had many conversations about the fact that I don't want to be the sole person responsible for what happens spiritually in the home. If she feels that we need to be praying more, I don't want her to assume I can read her mind; I want her not only to say it but also to drive it.

Amy: Another example would be the choice to get my MBA rather than making the default choice to immediately start having kids. Jon is so gung ho about this. He loves how happy and empowered it makes me. He's never threatened by me, not even by my making more money than he does. This is not typical. When I went back to school and kept working full-time, Jon took over all of the chores that I used to do. I feel no guilt. His choice to be so supportive and sacrificial has empowered me and given me hope rather than making me feel cursed because I have a dual passion for home and profession. This is perhaps the very reason that I married Jon.

As I've watched Jon and Amy during the course of their marriage, it's impossible not to notice their camaraderie and respect for each other. There's also an unmistakable ease, in part because they've learned how to accept their strengths as good gifts. I wish Christopher and I had figured this out earlier in our marriage. We clung to our expectations far too long, causing unnecessary strife.

I no longer want to judge, moralize, or see Christopher as a home-improvement project. I want to fully love and respect him. In order to achieve this goal, I must continually let go of my unbiblical expectations and bless the unique ways he reveals the image of God *as he is* rather than try to make him conform to my vision of who I think he *should be.* This process has been more difficult and humbling than I ever imagined, but I now have a deeper appreciation of his—and God's—profound otherness.

Going Deeper

1. Are there any areas where you feel as if you don't measure up to traditional gender norms? How has that shaped you? What areas of nontraditional gifts have been perceived as deficits or welcomed as assets in your marriage?

2. Do you feel permission to grow in or explore a role, chore, or job traditionally associated with the opposite gender? If not, why?

3. Do you reject or welcome your spouse's otherness? Write down five traits you admire, and be intentional about telling him or her this week. Make this a regular practice in your marriage. If you chafe at his or her otherness, write down the top three bothersome traits and ask God to give you more grace and help you to see His intentions in this otherness.

4. Prayerfully ask God if it would be helpful for you to apologize and repent for any areas where you have judged your spouse simply because of his or her confounding otherness. Rather than being a fault-finder, see if you can become a blessing-finder.

4

AN UNLIKELY
BLESSING

Mining Disappointment and Anger

Months before our tenth anniversary, I began to daydream about our upcoming celebratory getaway. We would eat dinners by candlelight, give each other extravagant presents, walk along the beach, and of course make love each night. As Christopher has learned, I'm fluent in all five love languages,[1] and on important events, such as birthdays and anniversaries, I want to experience as many as possible. When the weekend finally arrived, I was nearly giddy as we drove away.

That lasted about three hours. I was so eager to receive his gift that not long after we settled into the bed-and-breakfast, I suggested we exchange presents. He slid his hand into his bag and pulled out— wait for it—a card and a pen and sat down to write. On the day of our anniversary. I watched him and thought, *Ten years wasn't enough time to prepare for this date?* My giddiness morphed into anxiety.

He wasn't *un*prepared: he had written a poem for me. As he began to read it, my emotions tangled around themselves like a ball of discarded fishing line. My inner dialogue went something along the lines of *A poem? I wasn't expecting a poem. I wanted something tangible. How could he not know that? After ten years, he still doesn't understand me.* I tried to rally but failed. He countered with justifiable anger. Instead of joyfully kicking off our second decade, this weekend began a painful and disconcerting year. (Just for the record, I've repented for my selfish ingratitude.)

Though we were not conflict rookies, the intensity and stickiness of our anger unnerved us. It was as if this single event somehow epitomized every deficit in our marriage. Month after month, we hunkered down in our foxholes and lobbed verbal grenades at each other. After almost a year of this unproductive behavior, we reached out to wise friends for help. Without being aware of it, we had been minimizing and avoiding our disappointment and anger. As a result, we never learned what these feelings were trying to teach us and endlessly looped around the same half-dozen fights. Sound familiar?

In the context of marriage, if we find ourselves habitually disappointed and angry, we have four options: divest and/or quit, pretend that everything is fine (which is dishonest), try to change our spouses (which never works), or ask God to use the anger and disappointment to transform us so we can love our spouses independent of their behavior. If we want our marriages to thrive, we really only have one choice.

How do we arrive at that final option? First, we need to make a paradigm shift. We often assume that disappointment and anger indicate there's something wrong with us, our spouses, or our marriages. Such conclusions may cause us to feel shame and, as Mike Mason points out, "to pull back from the full intensity of the relationship, to get along on only the basic requirements."[2]

In order to give more of ourselves rather than pull back, we need to reframe anger and disappointment as holy invitations rather than dire pronouncements. Then, as we press into these disquieting feelings, we can accomplish three important objectives: discern what drives them, decipher the message they intend to communicate, and develop reality-based expectations.

Recognizing and Unpacking Disappointment

Disappointment can be nebulous. It sometimes manifests as sadness, irritability, fear, or despair, making it difficult to identify. Marital disappointment often surfaces in connection to what our spouses have or have not done. We feel disappointed because they stopped exercising and gained weight, disappointed that they cannot break free from depression, disappointed that they do not want to pray regularly. Though we can experience disappointment in our own failures and limitations, it's much easier to fixate on our spouses'.

At its core, "disappointment is an initial response to learning that our expectations will not be met."[3] Early on in our marriage, I was disappointed that Christopher did not share my enthusiasm for romance. He was disappointed that I had such difficulty staying engaged in lengthy conversations. Once we realize the connection between disappointment and expectations, choosing to remain in a place of disappointment "constitutes a failure to accept and grieve the loss of those expectations. By not accepting the losses, we perpetuate unhealthy disappointment."[4]

Apparently I have resisted accepting my losses because disappointment has been a faithful companion for most of my life. It has consistently robbed me of joy, perhaps specifically in my marriage. That anniversary fight? Because I came into the weekend with rigid expectations (I wanted flowers, a thoughtful card, and a unique gift), I was unable to appreciate my husband's offering. The disappointment that washed over me that afternoon quickly morphed into fear and despair. I assumed, *This dynamic will never change. We'll always miss each other on these milestone events.* Ironically, the traditional tenth-anniversary present is tin or aluminum, symbolizing the flexibility that marriage requires of us.

The Role of Disappointment in Ferreting Out Unhelpful Expectations

When we experience disappointment in marriage and it's no one's fault (such as a miscarriage or loss of employment due to corporate downsizing), we generally grieve and figure out how to move on. It's the disappointments that point back to our unrealistic expectations for each other that tend to be stickier. These hard-to-shake disappointments can sometimes be described as disordered attachments[5]—misplaced desires that compete with God for our heart. By following the thread that runs through our disappointments and our persistent anger, we can uncover their origin.

Christopher and I have had our share of sticky disappointments; that's part of what our year-ten crisis was all about. When I married him, naive optimism overshadowed the reality that he is mercurial, does not like public displays of affection, hates flying on airplanes, and has time-deficiency disorder. (Don't bother looking this up; I diagnosed him.) That same optimism obscured the reality that I struggle to need him, am too quick to judge, and prefer doing to talking.

These relational speed bumps were definitely not marked with fluorescent orange paint or signage of any sort. After we scraped our undercarriage and experienced whiplash more times than I care to admit, it began to dawn on us that perhaps we needed to find a more productive, less destructive path through our disappointments. We took a similar approach to how we unpacked our gender expectations by asking probing questions such as, *What if rather than blaming each other for our disappointments, we confessed our failures and owned our areas of weakness? What if we looked under the disappointments to discern if they revealed any egocentric expectations, disordered attachments, or misplaced hopes?* Once we stopped avoiding these seemingly problematic feelings and started investigating them, something shifted.

Rather than continuing to blame Christopher for my disappointment, I started asking the Lord to help me do three things: repent of any unfair expectations, appreciate Christopher's strengths, and develop reality-based expectations. Of these three objectives, developing reality-based expectations has been the most difficult. My unrealistic expectation of being romanced died an ugly, slow death because I stubbornly clung to it. Clinging is a form of denial that masquerades as hope. We persist in clinging because it gives us something to hold on to and allows us to sidestep the hard work of changing what we have control over: ourselves.

My prayers are finally paying off. I'm learning to let go of my unrealistic expectations by choosing an internal posture of holy resignation. Practically speaking, *holy resignation* means accepting and loving your spouse without demanding that he or she change, resisting the vortex of despair and blame, and standing in faith that God will complete a good work in the marriage—regardless of current circumstances.

Even as I mourned the death of my illusion, I gradually began to understand that it was my culturally informed expectations— not any actual deficits—that kept my disappointment on life support. (To clarify, it's not wrong to express our hopes and desires to our spouses or even ask them to develop in previously undeveloped areas. When it becomes clear that they will not or cannot meet our expectations, we have to adjust those expectations.) As I reflect back on this dynamic, I now realize that God had been inviting me to see from His vantage point for years, but I obstinately resisted and continued to blame Christopher for my unhappiness. That resistance loomed like a dark cloud over our relationship and eventually exploded into an angry storm on our tenth anniversary.

Learning to Recognize Anger

Throughout my adolescence and early twenties, whenever I walked past a cart of glass tchotchkes at the mall, I felt the overwhelming desire to smash them with a baseball bat. I had no idea what motivated this disconcerting impulse. One day while shopping with a friend, I casually mentioned my destructive fantasy. She furrowed her brows and said, "You need to pray about that."

Anger is part emotion and part primal physiological response. It can be triggered by an actual or perceived threat, an emotional hurt, someone's sin, coming face-to-face with our limitations, or by encountering injustice. Anger tends to accumulate, which is one of the reasons the apostle Paul advises, "Do not let the sun go down on your anger" (Eph. 4:26 NRSV).

In terms of physiology, anger and fear are closely linked. When we perceive a threat, our brains trigger a flight, freeze, or fight response. Heart rates soar, breathing quickens but becomes shallow, blood is diverted from organs less necessary for survival (e.g., the stomach), focus narrows—all in less time than it takes to read this sentence. Some enjoy the anger rush and chase after it because they find it stirs them to action or clarifies their thoughts. Others find the rush so intimidating that they do everything in their power to avoid it.

Religious barriers can contribute to our hesitancy to admit or express anger. As the authors of *The Cry of the Soul* state, "In many circles, passionate emotions are discouraged as unspiritual."[6] Like my family of origin, some church people conceal their anger under a veneer of niceness, perpetuating the myth that good Christians don't get angry (that myth is quickly dispelled if you scroll through Facebook during an election season).

My Mediterranean husband views anger through a different lens than most white North American believers. When our sons were young, we searched many books for wisdom to help us navigate perplexing discipline issues. After plowing through several, Christopher said, "Don't buy another parenting book written by a northern European author! I'm so weary of these emotionally reserved men telling me that only bad parents get angry at their children." A bit hyperbolic, but you get his point.

Unless we pathologically detach from relationships, politics, and current events, avoiding anger is impossible. Furthermore, if we're awake and paying attention, there's plenty going on that should cause righteous outrage, from racial inequality to corporate financial mismanagement to Christians acting reprehensibly toward other human beings and then claiming that God is on their side. Even if we lived in the Alaskan wilderness without Wi-Fi, our anger fuses would still get tripped.

Because we are all sinful men and women—married to sinful spouses—we should expect to occasionally feel disappointment and anger in our marriages. Christopher and I are reasonably self-aware, thoughtful people. We also have a few annoying habits and seemingly incompatible expectations that result in conflict. Take the passing of time, for example.

Christopher and I experience time differently. For me, it's finite and to be obeyed. For him, it's infinite and optional. In addition to our paying jobs (Christopher works as a teacher and worship leader, and I divide my time between writing and photography), we counsel individuals and couples. If you sit down with me for an hour-long appointment, I'm focused on the conversation but also aware of the clock. After my internal sundial registers fifty minutes, I will begin edging the meeting to a close. If you sit down with him, he's also fully present, so much so that time seems to stop. This works to your advantage if you're his first or second appointment but becomes a disadvantage if you're his fifth—or if you happen to be the spouse waiting for him to come home for dinner. When he calls to say he's leaving work, I've learned to ask for clarification: "Define leaving. Is your browser still open, or are the keys in the ignition?" Assuming the former, I have more than an hour to decide how to manage my swirling emotions.

Can I overlook his lateness, or do I let my frustration go from simmer to full boil as I finish making dinner? What happens the moment he walks through the back door? Do I voice my anger or simply welcome him home with a smile and a kiss? For those of you who feel comfortable expressing anger or having quickies (fights, not sex), you would probably be able to admit your feelings and move on. For those like me who have a complicated relationship with anger, it seems prudent to swallow our feelings and pretend all is well. Long term, this never works. The suppressed anger ferments into a sour indigestion that leaks out at the most inopportune moments. Such as tenth anniversaries.

It would be much better for our marriage if I could simply verbalize my frustration and then let it go. (Truth be told, it would be better if I could become less German in my understanding of time.) Instead, I second-guess whether it's okay for me to be angry, somehow assuming I should be able to rise above it. But where does that assumption originate? After all, isn't righteous anger a hatred of sin? Author and theologian Sarah Sumner boldly states in *Angry Like Jesus*, "When we lack Jesus' anger, we allow evil to prevail."[7] Jesus displayed anger when He encountered the money changers in the temple (Matt. 21:12), and "a deep anger welled up within him" when Lazarus died (John 11:33). Because of His intimate connection to God the Father and the Holy Spirit, Jesus was able to exhibit anger without descending into sin. As mere mortals, we don't always fare so well.

Five Anger-Based Responses

In order to learn the lessons that anger intends to teach us, we first need to recognize it. Christopher is much more adept at this than I am. Within seconds of his internal software flipping the switch, he understands exactly what's going on. Because he doesn't filter his anger as I do, his body has congruence with his emotions: he gets loud, his neck veins bulge, and I swear he grows several inches taller. Some of us sink into discouragement or depression. Some self-medicate with food or alcohol. Some of us grasp for control. I often hide behind sarcasm. If we are unable or unwilling to acknowledge our anger, sometimes our bodies do it for us. Temporomandibular joint disorder (often referred to as TMJ), back and neck aches, high blood pressure, and other somatic symptoms may point to repressed anger.[8]

Our personality types, our families of origin (and other cultural factors), and our past experiences all contribute to how we respond to anger. In broad strokes, we either project our anger outward or direct it inward—or both. As you could probably guess from what I've shared so far, I'm an innie and Christopher is an outie. Because

I know I'm not the only one who struggles to recognize anger, I'll present five familiar responses.

1. Defensiveness

Perhaps our most common anger response is to defend ourselves and blame others. Early on in our marriage, whenever I got mad at Christopher, I unintentionally channeled the voice of his disapproving mother, which triggered his shame and fear of incompetence. To push off from those unpleasant feelings, he would immediately defend himself and point out how I contributed to the problem. Because pushing back made me uncomfortable, I shut down. Though neither of us understood what was happening, his defensiveness became his trump card that kept me in place and prevented him from accepting responsibility. People who defend and blame typically fail to see their contribution to the situation and often have an overly complex relationship with criticism.

2. Moralizing

Those who moralize (and often judge) love to communicate that their preferences and opinions are the only valid choices. Think talk radio. As I mentioned in chapter 2 regarding ethnic differences, moralizing happens reflexively and we are often completely oblivious that we are doing it. Scout's honor—I had no idea I was moralizing until the eighty-ninth time Christopher brought it to my attention. When we moralize, we avoid our own shame by shaming others.

3. Manipulating

Early in our marriage, as soon as I noticed Christopher's neck veins bulging, I would become uncharacteristically agreeable in an effort to placate his anger. This strategy sometimes delayed the conflict but, in the end, exacerbated it because his manipulation antenna was as precisely tuned as my anger antenna. I manipulate when I sense there's a power differential and assume I have no legitimate options to get my point across.

4. Withdrawing

Withdrawers have a felt need to avoid or deny relational tension. They may manifest as peacemakers, working overtime to diminish differences and de-escalate conflicts. Though their efforts occasionally help, they can aggravate the situation long term because the underlying issues get pushed aside for the sake of false peace and then never get addressed. Fear often precedes withdrawal.

5. Lashing Out

Lashing out is increasingly common in our culture. Because so much of today's communication happens electronically, we lack the normal restraints and accountability that accompany face-to-face dialogue. It's all too easy to spout off when we can hit Send, close the computer, and smugly detach. When this style of processing anger happens within a marriage, trust erodes and fear gains a foothold. (Please note: If the anger in your household ever escalates to the point where you feel unsafe, please get help.)

We pick and choose from the problematic responses listed above to avoid feeling foolish, ashamed, or overly vulnerable; to avoid losing control or losing the relationship; and to avoid being wrong. If we hit the pause button as soon as we realize we're reacting, we can start to discern what's provoking our anger, address the causality, and learn to respond differently.

What Our Anger Is Trying to Tell Us

Anger is so compelling and all-encompassing that we can forget that the point of anger is not anger; the emotion is meant to get our attention so that we can learn something and mature. According to author Harriet Lerner, "Our anger may be a message that we are being hurt, that our rights are being violated ... or that ... our beliefs ... [are] being compromised."[9] Despite the discomfort that often accompanies anger, it can be "a surgical weapon, designed to destroy ugliness and restore beauty. In the hands of one who is trained in love and who can envision beauty, the knife of righteous anger is a weapon for restoration."[10] In order for us to reap the restorative benefits of anger, we need to tune in to the Holy Spirit.

One of the most helpful lessons I've learned in my thirty-five years of following Jesus is to pay attention to thoughts and behaviors that are inconsistent with my faith. My friend's response to my glass-smashing fantasy clued me in to the reality that my horizon was tilting. As soon as I was willing to explore this in the presence of the Lord, it became obvious that He had something to say. Over the next several months as I prayed, I began to realize that because I had dismissed my anger for so long, I no longer recognized it. The impulse to destroy something was my subconscious communicating that I was angry and needed to stop denying that reality.

Denying anger came naturally to me in part because I never saw it modeled well. When I was a teen, the one time I overtly expressed anger toward my parents resulted in having a bar of Ivory soap shoved into my mouth and an afternoon spent in solitary confinement. That was conventional wisdom at the time and hardly worth calling the Department of Social Services over, but the experience led me to conclude that if I was honest about my anger, it would result in my being punished and abandoned. Therefore, I assumed I should avoid anger at all costs, even if that meant lying.

Christopher's childhood anger had more to do with not being listened to or understood by his family and his peer group. He had few advocates who made the effort to know and support him. His anger became a form of personal identity and a source of power in the face of his powerlessness.

Your anger will undoubtedly have different origins than ours. Perhaps it's due to a fresh betrayal, connected to feelings of abandonment because of your spouse's compulsive work habits, or in response to unrelenting criticism. Please don't make the same mistake that I did and ignore your anger for decades. Recognize it, discern what it's trying to teach you, and then learn to express it constructively.

What Constructive Anger Looks Like

The raw power and strength of our angry feelings might lead us to assume we cannot control ourselves when we are angry. Sarah Sumner counters that thought: "To assert that human emotions are primarily biological—and not volitional and moral as well—is to promote a Freudian ethic of nonresponsibility."[11] The challenge is discovering how to be honest about our anger and expressing it in a healthy, nondestructive manner.

If you're an outie, like my husband, you might need to learn techniques that allow you to have a greater level of self-control. For some, that will mean being still before the Lord (Ps. 37:7–8) and awaiting His directive. Others might need a different tactic. Recent research has proved that when angry, if we can step back and engage our large muscles, we can interrupt the body's automatic response and gain objectivity.[12] That's why going for a walk, playing an instrument, making pottery, or vigorously vacuuming the house can help us think more clearly.

Those of us who are innies need to learn how to break through the fear attached to anger. After I explored my impulse to destroy the tchotchkes, I had a radical idea: *What if I smashed glass in a manner that would allow me to acknowledge and express my anger without hurting anyone or destroying anything of value?* I bought two dozen cheap drinking glasses; went to a neglected, glass-strewn spot; put on a pair of safety goggles; and hurled the glasses against a rock ledge. I certainly wouldn't recommend throwing things in your kitchen as spontaneous therapy (as in EVER!), but it was important for me to physicalize the anger that had been locked inside for three decades. Since my glass-smashing session—and because I'm trying to be more honest about my anger—mall tchotchkes no longer trigger destructive fantasies.

Regardless of what works best for you, it's of utmost importance to balance self-control with self-expression. Denial is not the same as self-control. Self-control, which includes being slow to anger and not being overtaken by anger, allows us to be honest without hurting ourselves or anyone else. If we do lash out, we need to take responsibility for the consequences of our anger. This emotion does not entitle us to mistreat others, especially our spouses and children, who are the closest to us and therefore the most likely targets.

Lessons Learned

Once we become facile in recognizing and communicating our anger, we discover what's causing all that clanging under the hood. As Christopher and I processed our tenth-anniversary fiasco, we noticed some unhealthy patterns. For one, my expectations felt crushing to him and contributed to his shame. Because I did not believe I had permission to directly address my disappointment and anger, I moralized my preferences, tried to manipulate him, and lied about what I was feeling. In turn, he felt he had no recourse but to defend himself. Though we freely shared our feelings with each other, we made little or no progress until we got to the point of deciding, *That's enough. We can't continue like this.*

Discovering that fight pattern offered us a glimmer of hope. After acknowledging that our default behaviors were failing us, we had to find other options. Initially, I assumed I could solve the problem by no longer wanting anything from Christopher. As if! The goal in marriage should not be to cut ourselves off from desire. "In fact, ignoring our desires may serve as the convenient way we remain ignorant and resist change."[13] The goal is to allow Jesus to convert our desires—for our longings to come into alignment with His desires for us and for our marriages.

The conversion of our desires seldom happens quickly or effortlessly. Instead, it comes through patient persistence, through a thousand incidental decisions to move closer to one another, and through ongoing dialogue with God. One of the most helpful tools in this journey of change is prayer, particularly the Lord's Prayer. Jen Pollock Michel writes,

> To pray "your kingdom come, your will be done," we express our desire (and God's!) that he rule over every corner of our lives.... To pray the prayer for the kingdom coming, we face the inevitability that our desires must be subordinated to God's. Kingdom prayers grow in us the will to belong more fully to God.[14]

Submitting our desires to the Lord so that they—and we—might be transformed is our life's work. Though we long to leave all of our brokenness and sin in the baptismal tank when we are pulled upward through the water, our habits stubbornly cling to us like wet clothes. The hoped-for changes in my life have taken what feels like an eternity to bear fruit.

We continued to have unpleasant, conflictual anniversaries and birthdays for years after our tenth anniversary. In fact, it wasn't until the Holy Spirit convicted me of my ungraciousness and stubbornness that the dynamic began to change. Although it was by no means wrong for me to want romance, it was unhelpful for me to demand it on my terms. We know we're not done working on this issue, but at least we now feel the wind at our backs.

Matt and Li's Story

Matt and Li are a passionate, highly communicative, interracial couple. They are two of the smartest, most intentional people I know. Matt and Li courageously agreed to talk about navigating disappointment and conflict within marriage. I asked them to start by describing disappointment.

> **Li:** I'm sure it looks like anger because everything looks like anger for me. If I feel disappointed, I get angry first.

> **Matt:** I come from a stiff-upper-lip family where we don't express much. My first reaction to disappointment is to just suck it up. This

philosophy generated a lot of depression and anger.

Li: One of Matt's ongoing disappointments is my lack of neatness. I don't feel capable of keeping things the way he likes it.

Matt: It's difficult for me that Li finds it challenging to contain her work here in the home. I need a level of order so that I can do what life asks of me.

Li: On my end, the disappointment centers on how differently our work and life has played out. When we first got married, we were both doing campus ministry. I had this dream that we'd work part-time and co-parent. Ultimately, that's not what Matt wanted. I've needed to let him take a different direction professionally and that has brought lots of little disappointments.

One of the recent topics in my spiritual-direction class was disordered attachments. I saw how I attached my sense of worth to my accomplishments rather than to God. The leader was essentially encouraging us to examine our negative emotions, such as disappointment, and trace them back to see if there's a disordered attachment at the other end. If that's the case, then what would a healthy attachment be? In the deep disappointments of my life, I do attach to my sense of identity, my hopes and dreams, and my desire for control. At the core, all of the disordered attachments were about holding on to my version of how I wanted life to go so that my dreams could be maximized.

Matt: I have my own ideas about how things should be done. In the beginning of our relationship, Li's disappointment was in part due to the fact that I would not agree with everything she wanted. If one spouse decides what life is going to be like without agreement from the other, there's going to be disappointment and conflict.

Li: We do have a high level of conflict. One of the ongoing dynamics is that when Matt expresses his frustration, I get defensive. I'm frustrated that he's frustrated. Then he feels unheard and nothing gets solved. It's a classic fight pattern. It's very hard for me not to defend myself when I feel criticized, in part because I fear that I will lose my voice.

Matt: This dynamic is so much better than it used to be. In the early days, we couldn't disengage and we'd go to bed angry. Now we know to take a time-out, but we always come back and resolve the conflict.

Li: One of the main disciplines that has helped us navigate our disappointments and conflicts has been our morning prayer ritual. After we had one heinous fight, Matt suggested that we try praying together every morning for just two minutes. We bless each other and then end with the Lord's Prayer. We've done this for thirteen years now. It's been transformational. It might not seem like much, but that two minutes gives God room to do some miraculous stuff.

Matt: And God has done miraculous stuff. I used to worry about how I would look to those in Li's Asian community. I don't have to fight to be me anymore. This is who I am, and we have a powerful marriage and great kids. Engaging with Li over the long haul and inviting God into this area of our relationship have changed me. Our challenges and conflicts have prepared me to do my professional work well. I now have more emotional intelligence.

Li: Our conflicts have also helped me to grow. My key disordered attachment is my addiction to my own significance and how I find that through achievement and performance. When I had kids and had to cut back my hours, I couldn't get that drug anymore. In those early years, I felt disappointment with Matt and with myself. But that's when I finally received Jesus's forgiveness. God took me to the wilderness so that I could see my idols. He then set me free to understand that the gift I can receive is Jesus and the kingdom of God, not what I can do for the kingdom.

The goal is freedom. When we're not disordered, we can live in the identity that we're God's beloved. Without having a challenging marriage, I doubt I would have received this gift.

Similar to what God has done in Matt and Li's marriage, God has been helping Christopher and me move beyond the constriction of disappointment and anger. Our changed dynamic is evident and welcome. It has allowed us to appreciate each other more fully and give ourselves more freely. As proof of this progress, for my fiftieth birthday, Christopher organized a magnificent party complete with fresh flowers, "Dorothy Trivia," and best of all a gluten-free and dairy-free potluck. It was a marvelous evening made all the sweeter because he not only initiated the celebration but also clearly intended to romance me. (He succeeded!) The kingdom has broken into our marriage, and by His mercy it will continue until He calls us home.

Going Deeper

1. Are you aware when you feel disappointed, or is the feeling camouflaged by other emotions and reactions? What's your default behavior when you are disappointed?

2. Name a familiar disappointment in your marriage. Are you able to discern what the disappointment is attached to? Does your spouse agree with your assessment? If the attachment is disordered, what would a healthy attachment look like? How could you make this transition from disordered to healthy attachments?

3. Are there any places in your marriage where it would be helpful for you to assume a posture of holy resignation (acceptance and hope without bitterness or judgment)?

4. What did your family of origin teach you about anger and conflict? (If you never witnessed your parents fighting, that's worth noting.) Were you allowed to express anger? If so, what methods of expressing anger were acceptable?

5. Of the five options for expressing anger, what's your preferred option? What's your spouse's? What goes on for you when your spouse gets angry at you?

6. How would you rate your ability to have constructive conflicts in real time rather than rehashing something you felt a month ago? How might this improve?

5

TUNING IN

Why Good Listeners Make Better Spouses

When Christopher and I decided that our dating relationship was serious enough to warrant an introduction to my father, we packed up my Subaru and headed to New Jersey. As we approached the New York state line, I realized that Christopher had talked almost non-stop through two states. I turned to him and said, "You know, I'm starting to feel like a tree, as if it doesn't really matter to you whether I'm listening or not. I know you're aware of my presence because the car is moving and you're not driving, but it doesn't seem as though my thoughts and opinions matter." After an awkward pause, he said, "You're correct." And then finished his story. That exchange left me wondering if our vastly different styles of communication would become an issue later on. (Short answer: yes. See below.)

Christopher has an enviable command of the English language. He's witty, precise, and persuasive. But because he's a verbal processor, he sometimes travels through a circuitous labyrinth of words to figure out what he thinks, holding me hostage along the way.

My preferred style of communication is to use the fewest words possible. I constantly edit my thoughts before opening my mouth, assuming others will grow impatient or bored if I talk too long. That economy of words makes for excellent tweets but can come off as intimidating or even brusque.

Because Christopher and I use words for a living, it would be easy to assume that we never struggle to effectively communicate with each other. Truth be told, we've struggled a lot. Many factors contribute to this, including our families of origin and our strong personalities. He grew up in a loquacious household where word count trumped listening. I grew up in a stoic family where much was left unsaid. After we took a personality test in premarital counseling, our pastor drew in a deep breath and tried his best to soften the news that we were off the chart in opposite directions on several key traits. There have been many times when we've wondered if our struggle to communicate well was unique to us or common to all married couples.

God demonstrated the power of words by speaking the universe into existence *ex nihilo*—making something from nothing. He set humanity apart from all other created beings by giving us the gift of speech. Because we are made in God's image, we too have the capacity to use words for life-giving, creative purposes.

Unfortunately, our use of language sometimes falls woefully short of God's intention. Husbands and wives can spend hours talking and not move one inch closer to really loving, appreciating, or understanding each other. Author Ann Voskamp believes, "Love isn't a function of communication so much as Love's a function of *communion*."[1] One of the ways husbands and wives can move beyond simple communication into a place of intimate communion is to open their hearts to God and each other through the act of sacred, or spiritual, listening.

Unlike hearing, sacred listening doesn't happen automatically. Adam McHugh writes in *The Listening Life*, "Hearing is an act of the senses, but listening is an act of the will…. Listening is about more than straining to hear voices; it's about preparing the conditions of our hearts, cultivating an openness inside us. In this way, listening is a *posture*, one of availability and surrender."[2]

In order to cultivate this kind of relational spaciousness with our spouses, we have to push through external and internal barriers (such as distractions and selfishness) and choose to be physically, emotionally, and spiritually present. When we succeed, we impart value and worth to our spouses, which is healing in and of itself. Listening then becomes "a fundamental means by which we … fulfill the call to honor others above ourselves."[3]

But that's not all. As we honor our spouses by listening, our reactions to their stories sometimes reveal areas of resistance and sin within us. Sacred listening gives the Holy Spirit room to bring conviction, thus transforming the one speaking and the one listening. As we grow in our willingness and ability to listen to each other, our hearts will soften and our love will grow exponentially.

Stiff Competition

Most of us listen at 25 percent of our capacity.[4] Christopher and I occasionally dip below that mark. The following two scenarios happen more often than I'd like to admit. Scenario number one: It's the middle of a workday. Christopher has a rare break and calls to check in. Because I'm an introvert who cringes every time the phone rings, I'm instantly at war with myself. Do I pick up but continue to edit, hoping he fails to notice the faint click of the computer keys? Or do I put the computer on sleep and walk out of the room so I can fully engage? Scenario number two: It's late in the evening. The chores are done, the dog has been walked, and the two of us collapse on the couch. Before I can formulate a single sentence, he opens his laptop, *just to check*. Half an hour later, he's still checking. I give up and go to bed. Why is it so challenging for us to sacrifice our agendas in those moments and really listen to each other?

In our current culture, communication options are ubiquitous. We can reach out and connect in a myriad of ways, including Skype, email, and text. Information bombards us from the moment we wake up until the moment we fall asleep, and even then, more than 65 percent of us keep our devices within an arm's length of our beds.[5] Disclaimer: I enjoy and rely on social media. It allows me to communicate efficiently and effectively. That said, though technology offers us unprecedented opportunities to share information, it can sometimes make it more difficult for us to truly listen to each other.

The next time you're in a public place, pay attention to how many couples are "alone together"[6]: physically present but emotionally distracted. We now accept that our real-life conversations might be interrupted by a text from the boss, an invitation to FaceTime with our offspring, or a trending hashtag. Technology has trained us to be impatient (slow Internet is inexcusable), not to prattle on (why take 200 characters when 140 will do?), and to value breadth over depth.

Numerous studies have shown that the average adult spends approximately ninety minutes a day engaged in leisure activities online. If you're spending that much time every day online, "there's got to be someplace you're not. And that someplace you're not is often with your family and friends."[7] Technology has hoodwinked us into believing that virtual face time will satisfy our relational needs more fully than actual face time. But does it? We should all be routinely asking ourselves if technology is serving us—or if we're serving it.

How Pain Avoidance, Fear, and Selfishness Affect Our Listening

It's not simply modern technology that limits our ability to listen. Due to any number of reasons, we sometimes turn away from rather than toward our spouses in the midst of their pain. This was true for me three years ago when Christopher and I sensed that we needed to leave the church where he had been on staff for more than fifteen years. Though we longed to stay, all of the indicators unequivocally confirmed that moving on was the only sane option.

Christopher's anguish, sense of betrayal, and hurt were palpable. After we said our good-byes to the congregation and packed up his office, the devastating reality of our choice began to sink in. For months we talked, cried, and prayed, but then something shifted in me. I knew he needed more time to deal with his losses, but I found myself growing increasingly impatient. In an effort to hurry him along, I started making suggestions about how to fix things rather than listening and empathizing. As I began to detach, he felt increasingly alone, which intensified his need to talk and made me feel more overwhelmed. Isn't this type of dynamic what drives some of our most frustrating conflicts within marriage and also within culture?

As it turns out, I was seeking to avoid both his pain and my fears. Fear of failure looms large for me. My perfectionistic tendencies incline me to be all things to all people, particularly my husband. If I failed to assuage Christopher's pain, would he get angry with me? Or worse, would he descend into depression? And then what? Because I didn't know what else to do, I selfishly pushed for solutions rather than prioritizing his need to process.

The tendency to fix rather than to simply be present in the face of powerlessness and pain is common, perhaps more so for men than women. According to author Dr. Gary Chapman, "Many of us … are trained to analyze problems and create solutions. We forget that marriage is a relationship, not a project to be completed or a problem to solve."[8] Trying to fix things gives us something concrete to do and offers us a momentary reprieve from our troublesome realities. In certain situations, it's actually possible to fix the problem and alleviate the pain. But when we default to this activistic behavior, we often miss what's more important: to know and love each other more fully and ease the inherent loneliness that all humans experience.

Our selfishness can become another very real impediment to easing this aloneness. Sometimes we want to be heard more than we want to hear. We want to be understood more than we want to understand. We want to be right more than we want to love.

To genuinely honor and love our spouses, we need to identify and dismantle the broken habits that block us from this goal. Christ shows us the way.

What Does Jesus Teach Us about Becoming Better Listeners?

Throughout Scripture, Jesus models sacred listening. His conversation with the woman at the well illustrates how transformational it can be. On their way to Galilee, Jesus and His disciples journeyed through Samaria. Based on the orthodox Jewish customs, this was an odd choice. Jews were so antagonistic toward the mixed-race Samaritans that they would normally go miles out of their way to avoid having any contact with them. As the apostles ventured off to find food, Jesus "sat wearily beside the well about noontime. Soon a Samaritan woman came to draw water" (John 4:6–7).

That's when things got interesting.

In Jesus's time, it was scandalous for rabbis to talk to a woman who was alone in public. When He asked the Samaritan woman for a drink, He toppled the prevailing ethnic and gender barriers. She understood that something unusual was happening and responded with, "You are a Jew, and I am a Samaritan woman. Why are you asking me for a drink?" (v. 9). Jesus somewhat cryptically replied, "If you only knew the gift God has for you and who you are speaking to, you would ask me, and I would give you living water" (v. 10).

After a brief discussion about Jacob's well and the promise of living water (Jesus was referencing multiple Old Testament passages that referred to Him as living water; see Jer. 2:13), Jesus took the conversation to a deeper level by going directly to the heart of the matter: her need for a Savior.

> "Go and get your husband," Jesus told her.
>   "I don't have a husband," the woman replied.
> (John 4:16–17)

Jesus applauded her honesty and said,

> You're right! You don't have a husband—for you have had five husbands, and you aren't even married to the man you're living with now. You certainly spoke the truth! (vv. 17–18)

In what seems to be a dodge of this confrontation, the Samaritan "keeps the conversation … on the surface, but Jesus listens into the hidden places sunk in her soul and brings her secret pain to the surface."[9] After Jesus revealed Himself as the Messiah, "the woman left her water jar beside the well and ran back to the village, telling everyone, 'Come and see a man who told me everything I ever did! Could he possibly be the Messiah?' So the people came streaming from the village to see him" (vv. 28–30). Several verses later, we see the fruit of their exchange:

> Many of the Samaritans from that town believed in him because of the woman's testimony. (v. 39 NIV)

How did this short conversation result in such a profound transformation? Jesus valued this woman and treated her with respect. He did not shame, dismiss, or take advantage of her. When she attempted to pull the conversation back to a less vulnerable place, He gently but firmly redirected her. Finally, after she admitted her sin, Christ revealed Himself to her. This exchange seemingly freed her from her shame and transformed her into a bold evangelist.

Levels of Listening

Maybe it's unfair to hold Jesus out as the model of how to listen well. How many of us have the requisite prophetic gift to understand what our spouses are thinking at any given moment? (Personally, I'm divided on whether or not that would be a good idea.) So what's the takeaway from Jesus's conversation with the woman at the well?

We can listen on three levels: passively, actively, or spiritually. Most of the time, we listen passively. Rather than give our full attention, we might avoid eye contact, mumble a quick response, or quickly disengage and return to our own thoughts. When we listen passively, we aren't expecting the conversation to evolve into anything more than a simple exchange of information.

When we listen actively, we become invested in the conversation. We make eye contact and move close enough for our bodies to touch. We also work to understand the content and the emotional impact of what's being said. Rather than biding our time until it's our turn to talk, we fully enjoy connecting. (And in our experience, this type of bonding often leads to great sex!)

The third level is what I refer to as sacred, or spiritual, listening. This is what Jesus did with the Samaritan woman. As our conversations flow, we're listening and simultaneously discerning what's happening on the spiritual plane—what the Holy Spirit might be saying. Does my spouse's tone clue me in to any hidden anger or bitterness? Do those tears communicate that we're touching some historic pain? The goal is to try to understand how the conversation might usher the kingdom of God into our marriages. Active and spiritual listening both demand that we tune out all other distractions and give ourselves fully to the present moment. Making the commitment to engage in active and spiritual listening at least once a day for ten to fifteen minutes will dramatically increase our trust, affection, and intimacy.

Why Self-Awareness Matters

In order for us to hone our listening skills and move from passive listening to active and spiritual listening, we need to have a basic understanding of who we are and how that relates to our spouses. For example, Christopher and I are tenacious, determined, and at times impatient. We are compulsively creative and addicted to finding God's beauty everywhere. We are learning to live in faith but still tend to doubt and fear. As mentioned, I have unrealistically high expectations and get disappointed easily. He battles shame.

Here's how those realities make it difficult for us to listen to each other as we're planning our vacation. Seven years ago, we successfully blocked off two weeks. I desperately wanted to go someplace beautiful near a large body of water. I had our financial constraints in the back of my mind, but they were in the way back, behind the boxes of Christmas ornaments in the attic. After far too many hours searching on the Internet, I found the perfect house with lots of light, a cook's kitchen, and a water view. Christopher felt it was too expensive and began his own search. He discovered a rustic cabin that sleeps eight and was suspiciously cheap. Cheap is his love language. As a compromise, we divided our vacation between those two sites.

When we arrived at the rustic cabin, we immediately realized the online description failed to disclose a few key details, such as rodent droppings. While putting away my suitcase, I discovered a hole in the exterior bedroom wall. This increased the airflow, which was important because the windows were nailed shut, but became slightly disconcerting after the sun went down. The supposedly well-stocked kitchen included only a bottle opener, a cheese grater, and a very dull knife. To Christopher's credit, there was a lovely little brook at the edge of the property.

What does all this have to do with self-awareness and listening? Lots.

Until our fourth trip, we didn't understand how our failure to listen to each other complicated everything. Christopher's fear of going over budget caused so much static that he could not hear my desperate need to escape our gritty urban life for a few weeks. I was not expecting a four-star hotel on Maui, but I was pushing our budget beyond his comfort level. My desires drowned out his legitimate concerns. We both lacked sufficient self-awareness to realize how we were missing and disrespecting each other.

Self-awareness means that we see our sin patterns, are grieved by them, and work to overcome them. It means we acknowledge our limitations and their cost to our spouses. To be self-aware is also to admit that we can't get past our sin and brokenness by sheer determination or intellectual prowess; we need Jesus. If you don't know what those areas of sin and brokenness are or how they influence your relationship, go ahead and ask your spouse—but not until you're ready to hear the answer.

The Role of Intentionality and Discernment in Becoming Better Listeners

Several years ago, our church's small-group pastor was teaching a workshop on listening. After a brief introduction, he summarized the first exercise. We were instructed to pair off in groups of two and have one person talk on any topic for ten minutes without interruption. The listener would then share with the speaker what he or she heard, in terms of actual and emotional content. The small-group pastor and I were paired together. I'll call him Michael. He went first.

Michael casually mentioned that he had been experiencing abdominal pain and, at his wife's urging, had finally gone in for some tests. Then he dropped the bomb. "It might be cancer." Momentarily stunned, I forgot the rules of the exercise and blurted out, "What? Please tell me you're kidding!" He wasn't. As I listened to him share this fresh news, we both started crying. By nature, Michael was a sanguine guy. I had never seen him shed tears or express anger. Perhaps a similar conversation would have evolved if we had bumped into each other after church, but I doubt it. Because he knew I was singularly focused on him, he felt enough safety to share his jagged, unguarded emotions. Tragically, it was cancer and it took his life in less than two years.

That morning was a game changer for me. I had assumed I was a good listener, but the exercise revealed my impatience and tendency to control conversations. Since then, I have been attempting to love Christopher and others by listening more attentively without inserting my thoughts, guiding the conversation, or giving advice.

Everyone's marriage would benefit by practicing this type of listening on a regular basis. Ten minutes might not seem sufficient, but we seldom listen to one another for that long without interrupting. I won't pretend that Christopher and I make a nightly discipline out of this, but at least during dinner and a few other times every week, we shut down our devices and give each other our undivided attention. By the way, don't be surprised if you encounter opposition as you embark on this. The Enemy strongly prefers that we remain disconnected and lonely.

In addition to becoming more intentional, we also need to grow in discernment. One of the most difficult aspects of becoming a good listener is learning to identify and understand what's happening on the different levels of every exchange: what actually occurred (or is occurring), your feelings, and what the conversation says about you (e.g., what's at stake).[10] In the example I shared about leaving the church we loved, what had happened was we'd come to a theological impasse with several members of the staff. What we felt was betrayal, sadness, and anger. What was at stake was the loss of employment, friends, and our faith community. Each level is highly subjective and loaded with potential land mines because though what happened seems obvious, our biases and wounds alter our perceptions.

To further develop your listening skills, try to (1) give introverts sufficient time to respond, (2) avoid the temptation to minimize or fix, and (3) ask open-ended questions that give your spouse permission to explore their feelings. The biggest payoff will come as we allow our spouses' words to penetrate our hearts and change us. This is exactly what has happened for Mateo and Sofia.

Mateo and Sofia's Story

Both from Spanish-speaking countries, Mateo and Sofia exude the warmth and charm so common among those from Latin cultures. He works as an engineer, and she is an entrepreneur with artistic leanings. Of all the topics in the book, the challenges of sacred listening resonated the most with them. I'll let them jump in.

> **Mateo:** There are two things that make this kind of listening difficult for me. First, we had a dictator running our country for many years. It's a very authoritative, machismo culture. How can you learn to ask questions and listen when that's your heritage? If I say to my family, "I feel sad

today," they would probably ask some general questions about how I'm doing but not go deep.

Second, Spanish men are passionate and vocal, but we don't focus on how we are feeling. If I'm angry, it would be difficult for me to describe why.

Sofia: In addition to the cultural elements, I was an only child and my mom was widowed when I was very young. I struggle with vulnerability because it wasn't modeled for me. Mateo is a solid guy, and if he falls apart, who will pick up the pieces? Ninety-nine percent of the time, he's a gladiator. When he shows vulnerability, I can be impatient.

Mateo: Then I feel as though I cannot be weak in front of her because if I'm weak, she tries to fix me. So I'll just push away and pray about what's going on. Sometimes that prayer is asking God, "What do You have to say?" My pattern of retreating is based on childhood dynamics. In my family, when there was a conflict among the siblings, everyone would get punished. I learned to go off by myself and figure out what happened.

Sofia: What's crazy about this is that when he goes away to try to figure things out, it does not help me because I want to solve the problem immediately. We're project managers. We're good at making lists and then checking things off. We get exhausted when it comes to trying to figure out how to listen patiently and love each other in our listening. One finite example of this struggle would be the fence around our property. Because we live in a crowded urban setting and had a theft in our house, I asked Mateo to put up a fence, but I was not involved in the design or planning process.

Mateo: I did my research and put the fence up, but the color and design didn't come out exactly as either of us wanted. She looked at the fence and then told me she wanted me to remove it.

Sofia: Aesthetics are so important to me, and this fence is not pleasing to look at. I can't detach from the visual component of it. And it's not just the visuals. It's symbolic of an ongoing issue for us that when I ask him to do something for me, we may have two separate priorities in mind. So the work gets done but it doesn't make both of us happy.

Mateo: Not surprisingly, I felt angry and misunderstood. I wanted her to see that the fence was a good thing, and I didn't want to hear her talk about it anymore.

They looked across the table at each other and then laughed, immediately diffusing the tension.

> **Sofia:** I do feel that we are making progress, but I also feel as though we're the Israelites, taking a long time and complaining when we don't really need to. Our faith has definitely helped on this journey. We've gone through lots of training to learn how to listen in prayer. When we do that for each other, it's powerful.

> **Mateo:** I agree. I think some of our most intimate times of listening to each other have happened through prayer. For the last year or so, I've also been trying to figure out what motivates me to listen or even do things for Sofia. Am I doing it for God or for myself? A good midwife is there for the mother-to-be. She's not dictating what's happening or forcing her agenda on the mother. I guess I'm learning to be a midwife as I listen so that it's about what Sofia needs rather than what I need.

Like Sofia and Mateo, Christopher and I continue to make discoveries when we engage in sacred listening. These discoveries typically happen when we push everything else to the margins, invite God in, and focus on each other. Obviously, not all of our conversations are holy, tender moments. We're often downloading information, interrupting, and missing opportunities to connect. Big picture: we've grown and we're committed to keep growing.

Though sometimes I still feel overwhelmed by the sheer volume of Christopher's words, I increasingly value his willingness to share his thoughts with me. Thankfully, he's learned to give me more time to figure out and articulate my feelings. And no small miracle, I now look forward to long car rides with him because of the opportunity they provide to commune with each other without being interrupted by buzzing gadgets or the ever-present pull of work. When Christopher occasionally gets stuck in a labyrinth, I simply tell him I'm feeling like a tree, and he gets it.

Going Deeper

1. Is there a good balance of listening and talking in your marriage? Does one of you tend to talk more? How does this affect your relationship? If you would like it to be more balanced, how could you make that happen?

2. What's your relationship like with electronic devices? Is it easy for you to put them away for stretches of time? Consider turning off your electronic devices for a set amount of time every day. See if this increases your ability to listen to each other. (And, please, keep them out of the bedroom. If you need an alarm, buy a clock.)

3. Think of three things you need from your spouse when you have a conversation (physical connection, to be asked follow-up questions, and so on). Is he or she aware of these needs? If not, how can you communicate them?

4. Call to mind a recent argument or difficult conversation you had with your spouse. Are you able to discern the three levels that were going on beneath the surface? In retrospect, what could have made this conversation go better?

6

UNMASKING COUNTERFEITS

How Disordered Attachments and Addictions Thwart True Desire

Sometimes God shows up in unexpected places. One of the most profound epiphanies I've ever experienced happened not in church but in the grocery store. In the months leading up to this, I noticed that I was obsessively thinking about food. I would plan the week's menu while listening to the sermon or stop at the market for a few items and emerge half an hour later with twenty. I subscribed to three food magazines and religiously read each issue. And no matter how much bread I ate, I always wanted more.

On this particular night, I allowed myself a moment of quiet reverie in the bakery section. After much deliberation, I chose two loaves of sourdough and lovingly set them on top of my overflowing cart. Moments later, while standing in the checkout line, I surveyed my merchandise. It was too much. Even with a family of five, I could not justify buying this much food. Feelings of shame and condemnation descended upon me.

In that vulnerable moment, I shot up a prayer to God: *What's going on with my out-of-control food shopping and the bread obsession?* He instant-messaged me with a question of His own: *What does food represent to you?* I burst into tears. The teenage checker eyed me with a combination of care and suspicion and inquired if I needed help. I nodded, then clarified, "Not the kind you would be able to provide."

Some of you might wonder why I would include this topic in a marriage book written primarily for Christians. Others completely understand but wish you didn't. I'm writing on disordered attachments and addictions because I agree with psychiatrist and counselor Gerald May, who writes,

> The psychological, neurological, and spiritual dynamics of full-fledged addiction are actively at work within every human being. The same processes that are responsible for addiction to alcohol and narcotics are also responsible for addiction to ideas, work, relationships, power, moods, fantasies, and an endless variety of other things. We are all addicts in every sense of the word.[1]

May's claim might come off as simultaneously hyperbolic and offensive. Does he really mean to indict all of us? I think so. Some of us are attached to inarguably destructive substances such as pornography and tobacco. Others of us have developed unhealthy relationships with media or food. All day, every day, we face an onslaught of temptations. When we repeatedly give in to these temptations, they sabotage our transformation, suck the life from our marriages, and prevent us from discovering our true desires.

Despite my conviction that this chapter needs to be included, it's not an easy one to write. Though it's now totally normal to disclose any and all personal details to the world via social media, I do not enjoy revealing the sins that Christopher and I battle. However, regarding sin, if we stay silent, we stay trapped. If we admit our struggles and failures, we are more likely to break the power of shame and self-deception. In order to become more like Jesus and love our spouses well, we need to root out all addictive thoughts and behaviors and learn to make healthy attachments. I'll talk about how that happens in this chapter.

What's So Bad about Sin? (And What Exactly Qualifies as Sin?)

We start the process of breaking free from disordered attachments and addictions when we willingly name certain thoughts and behaviors as sin. This tiny word carries powerful psychological and theological implications, which might be why we tend to avoid it. Most of us understand sin as either a debt incurred due to a specific failure (which Jesus repays through His death on the cross), or a soul-sickness (which Jesus heals), or both. According to theologian N. T. Wright, "'Sin' … is not 'breaking the rules' but 'missing the mark,' failing to hit the target of complete, genuine, glorious humanness."[2] Put more simply, sin is thoughts and behaviors that diminish us and prevent us from thriving.

Though we're all good people with good intentions, we all sin. I have repeatedly lied, hoarded my time, gossiped, and failed to care for widows and orphans. Christopher has succumbed to envy and gluttony, overused media, and trusted the work of his hands over God's provision. (Neither list is exhaustive.) These were not simply inconsequential mistakes. Because they were motivated by selfishness, fear, pride, and so on—all of which are contrary to God's nature—they need to be named for what they are: sin. And because sin separates us from God and each other, it must be included in our conversations about making our marriages beautiful.

Despite our current reality, it was not God's intention for sin to be part of marriage. Satan introduced enmity to the world by asking one simple question: "Did God really say you must not eat the fruit from any of the trees in the garden?" (Gen. 3:1). Obviously, the serpent was not earnestly seeking clarification. The question was meant to cast a shadow of doubt on God's character and simultaneously tear apart the first marriage. And as we all know, the scheme worked—not just for Adam and Eve but for all of humanity.

Today the Enemy asks each of us a similar question. Though the specifics vary, the first four words are always the same: "Did God really say …?" Perhaps he asks you, "Did God really say that you could experience sexual pleasure only in the confines of your marriage?" or "Did God really say that you can't indulge in romantic fantasies about someone other than your spouse?"

When we face ongoing temptations or have unfulfilled desires, we might begin to wonder if God's way really leads to an abundant life. Our doubt can be summed up in two questions: *Is He really a good and loving Father?* and *Can I trust Him?* If Adam and Eve had been able to answer yes to those questions, could they have sent the serpent packing? If the man viewing online porn believed that following Paul's advice to flee from sexual immorality (1 Cor. 6:18) would ultimately benefit him and his wife, could he close the browser and humbly ask for help?

Here's another more specific question directly connected to disordered attachments and addictions: *Is God's mandate for how we steward our bodies the exclusive way we will flourish?* Author David Platt responds in *Counter Culture*:

> The Bible emphasizes the importance of our bodies, saying that the body is meant "for the Lord, and the Lord for the body" (1 Corinthians 6:13). That simple phrase is a substantial starting point for understanding God's design for us. Our bodies have been created not only *by* God but also *for* God.[3]

If this is true, then only when we submit the whole of who we are to our Father's directives will we find true satisfaction, contentment, and joy.

We become familiar with those directives and gain understanding of the nature of sin by regularly reading and studying our owner's manual: the Bible. According to several vice lists found in the New Testament, the following fall under the category of sin: greed, theft, idolatry, jealousy, selfishness, pride, lying, as well as the many forms of sexual sin (1 Cor. 6:9–11, 18; Gal. 5:19–21).[4] And in case you don't find your specific sin listed, James 4:17 reads, "Remember, it is sin to know what you ought to do and then not do it."

What Do Addictions Look Like?

An addiction can be defined as a "state of compulsion, obsession, or preoccupation that enslaves a person's will and desire."[5] It is "a state of thirsting again and again for something that is not living water."[6] In other words, addictions will not—and by nature cannot—satisfy our true need. Patrick Carnes, in his classic book on addictions, *Out of the Shadows*, writes,

> Addiction taps into the most fundamental human processes. Whether the need is … to be sexual, to eat, or even to work, the addictive process can turn creative, life-giving energy into a destructive, demoralizing compulsivity.[7]

We can become addicted to almost anything, but none of us take the first bite of the apple aware of just how bitter the fruit will eventually become. Christopher initially encountered pornography in his uncle's garage at age twelve. Soon after, he began what would become a fifteen-year addiction to fantasy and masturbation. In addition to my unhealthy attachment to food, I spent hours poring over Pottery Barn, Williams-Sonoma, and other high-end decorating catalogs, imagining how my life would be quantifiably better if I had *that* house with *that* patio and *those* plates. It didn't matter whether or not I purchased anything. I wasted an inordinate amount of time coveting and not being grateful for my abundant life.

Because there's so much deceit swirling around addictions, we sometimes lack the objectivity necessary to identify them. Addictions have five stages: a triggering event or thought, preoccupation with the addiction, ritualization, the compulsive act, and finally, shame and despair.[8] (Whereas no stage model can be viewed as an absolute, a model like this one is useful when facing problems as large and complex as addiction.) Until we are willing to recognize the specific facets of our addictions, we may find ourselves stepping off the cliff before we realize where our feet have taken us.

In the first stage, a trigger might be as innocent as driving past a risqué billboard or hearing the pop of a cork as it's pulled from a wine bottle. It might also be more complex. Christopher's addictive cycle was often prompted by peer rejection, loneliness, or performance anxiety. Feeling sorry for myself and craving beauty typically initiated my compulsive-shopping fantasies.

Stage two of the addictive process is preoccupation. Whether it's shopping, eating, gambling, or acting out sexually, we begin to tune out other options and people as we move toward the object of our desires. Because what we're doing feels shameful, secrecy is imperative.

During the ritualization phase, we create special routines that safeguard the process, make it predictable, and prolong the enjoyment. The pornography addict might act out every

Saturday night. The woman trapped by the empty promises of hypersexualized romance novels might pour herself a glass of Merlot and always sit in the same chair whenever she reads.

Throughout the process, excitement builds even as we detach from reality, ignore potential consequences, and distance ourselves from our spouses and God. At this point in the cycle, it's nearly impossible to stop (though we tell ourselves and others that we could stop whenever we want). The pinnacle might be an orgasm, hitting the buy button, the first sip of alcohol, or the back-and-forth of potentially dangerous social media relationships. As soon as the euphoric moment is over, death and shame rush in, eclipsing the fleeting euphoria with the truth that we are trapped.

Steven is a talented, mature professional. His two-decade sexual addiction began while he was in college and gradually escalated from soft pornography to hard-core porn to strip clubs and, finally, to massage parlors. He was triggered by financial stress, too much unstructured time, and seeing sexually charged images (which are increasingly prevalent in our culture). Those triggers quickly placed him in the fast lane to the preoccupation and ritualization phases. He admits, "I had the whole city mapped out. I knew which bookstores had the most explicit stuff and which corner stores allowed easy browsing of magazines. When going grocery shopping, I would stop at a strip club and then shop. I had very specific routes." After acting out, Steven experienced "disgust, regret, anxiety, despair, and the terror of being discovered." This succinctly describes addiction's downward spiral.

What Causes Our Disordered Attachments and Addictions?

The causality of addictions is as varied as the ways we act out. Most addictions emerge as misguided attempts to meet genuine needs or alleviate pain. When we try to meet our needs and alleviate pain on our own, we may make disordered attachments. God designed us to attach to Him and healthy others. His intention is for us to turn to Him and these others whenever we experience need, desire, or pain. The Enemy continuously slips us counterfeits, hoping that we will attach to and depend on them. They woo us by approximating what we need, numbing our pain, and providing quick relief or even great pleasure. Counterfeits promise us everything but ultimately provide nothing.

That evening in the grocery store, the Holy Spirit's question pierced through this deception. What did the food, specifically the bread, represent? Something powerful that I lacked during those early years of parenting: nurture. Like any symbol, it pointed me to a deeper reality. And like any symbol, it had the potential to become a substitute for the actual object of my longing: true nurture offered by God, my husband, and my Christian brothers and sisters.

The thought processes and behaviors that lead us to choose counterfeits can be set in place early, long before we know what we are doing or why we are doing it. This proclivity toward addiction is not necessarily an indictment of our families. Even if we were raised in godly, intact homes, all of us experience anxiety, disappointment, pain, and loss. As children, if we faced these stressors on an ongoing basis or did not have help learning how to develop healthy strategies, we defaulted to coping. Some of the coping strategies we turned to were maladaptive, such as eating when lonely. Over time, it's possible for such behaviors to gradually devolve into addictions.

Numerous factors contribute to our maladaptive coping behaviors. Some factors—such as onetime traumas or repeated episodes of physical or sexual abuse—are obvious. Others are inconspicuous. Because I was unusually sensitive and felt things so deeply, I learned to hide my needs from others and take care of myself. Being a victim of racism and socioeconomic injustices can contribute to addictive behavior because powerlessness propagates desperation and despair. Some research points to genetics as a significant contributor to addictive behavior.[9] (It remains unclear how much of that is spiritual [see Deut. 5:9; Exod. 20:4–6] and how much is physiological.) Certain types of family systems may foster addictive patterns, specifically families that are chaotic or have "high demands for performance and achievement coupled with little or no encouragement and nurture."[10]

Another factor that inclines us toward disordered attachments and addictions is a failure to bond with our parents.[11] God sets us in families so that our emotional, physical, and spiritual needs will be consistently and lovingly met. Many of our mothers and fathers instinctively began the process of bonding as they nurtured us through gentle touch, a caring tone of voice, attentiveness, and the provision of physical sustenance. Our parents' consistent care communicated that we were lovely and lovable, which allowed us to feel secure and confident. A secure child does not dwell on fear of rejection or abandonment and understands how to connect, even at a young age.

If we failed to bond with our parents or caregivers, we may gravitate toward unhealthy behaviors and thoughts in an effort to alleviate the dull ache that lingers from our unmet needs. Insecure children might feel compelled to become perfect in hopes of avoiding criticism. They might learn to detach from their emotions and attach to objects that will not disappoint or hurt them, such as food, television, and books.

As maladaptive coping behaviors become habits, faulty belief systems develop around them. A faulty belief system may lead us to understand God as distant and harsh rather than accessible and loving. We may struggle to trust others and assume we have to take care of ourselves. This skewed set of beliefs also permeates our self-perception. We look at ourselves in a shattered mirror and see a defective version of reality rather than an accurate depiction of individuals who reflect a glorious God.

Broken cultures confirm our flawed beliefs rather than convicting us of our sin and pointing us back to God. In the United States, we bow down to the idols of power and distorted youthful sexuality. In this idolatrous landscape, "men become economic symbols. Women become sex symbols."[12] Culture encourages men to exploit their power in the boardroom and the bedroom and to brush aside their God-given calling as coheirs. In this system, women are objectified and then wrestle to make sense of two divergent distortions: first, that their bodies wield power because men want what they have; and, second, that they may be overtaken by men at any time and therefore are exceedingly vulnerable. Both genders are discouraged from controlling sexual urges, a tragic reality that diminishes all of us.

Rather than help us become fierce warriors and humble servants for the kingdom of God, broken cultural systems push us toward instant gratification. They encourage us to stuff our needy bodies with sugar, alcohol, and drugs instead of filling ourselves with the life-giving body and blood of Christ. They also aim to convince us that control is more advantageous than interdependence. If we buy into the lie that these broken systems offer, we turn our backs on our spouses and God and fall into the deceitful embrace of the counterfeit.

How Do Addictions Affect Marriages?

In God's design, our marriages are to be characterized by nurture, trust, vulnerability, sacrificial love, and intimacy. Sexual addictions, particularly those leading to infidelity, affect every one of these components. When a spouse goes outside of the marital covenant to get his or her sexual needs met, trust is destroyed and a sense of safety is lost. The betrayal may take years or even decades to heal. Regarding the repercussions of his addictions on his wife, Steven, whom I introduced a few pages back, said, "I will never fully grasp the depth of pain I caused Cassandra—the degree to which I betrayed her trust and shredded her self-esteem. Our former pastor described the impact of my addiction as 'that of a Mack truck driving though a beautiful stained-glass window.'"

The effect of sexual addictions and infidelity on the marital covenant is inarguable, but the truth is, *all* addictions adversely affect marriage. One spouse's addictive tendencies can create or foment an addictive response in the other person. For instance, when the husband is constantly plugged in and cannot detach from the virtual world, the wife may learn to cope with being ignored by finding a counterfeit of her own. If we increasingly turn outward to get our needs met, alienation, hopelessness, and anger may result. It's no surprise that this dynamic can make us vulnerable to affairs.

The damage from our addictive behaviors extends far beyond the relational component. Studies have shown that habitual use of pornography functions in much the same way that a milder, gateway drug does in the realm of addiction: it creates neural pathways or behavioral grooves that incline us toward the same type of pleasurable rewards. Repeated exposure to pornography can also lead to darker, riskier forms of sexual behavior, such as anonymous hookups and sadism/masochism.[13] Additionally, if we continue our addictive patterns, we will need increasing amounts to find the same level of relief.

Other forms of addictive behavior have their own unique repercussions. Scripture is quite clear about the concept of sowing and reaping: "Do not be deceived: God cannot be mocked. A man reaps what he sows" (Gal. 6:7 NIV). Though we might pretend that it isn't true, our behaviors have consequences that will affect not only our spouses but quite possibly generations to come. If we fail to deal with our addictions, our children may face similar struggles (see Exod. 20:4–6).

Finally, addictive behavior squanders our relational and creative energy. The time we spend hiding our forbidden stashes, devising virtual versions of ourselves, and fantasizing about the life we wish we had diverts us away from what God is calling us to do, as well as the actual family waiting for us at the dinner table. Investing our creativity in our marriages and in the pursuit of God brings a much more satisfying and lasting return, even though it involves considerably more effort.

Getting Free

Steven, Christopher, and I each took the first step toward freedom by confessing our sins. Not long after my epiphany at the grocery store, I felt the Holy Spirit communicating that I needed to tell someone. Rather than dismissing this terrifying thought, I told Christopher first and then a few close friends. It felt totally humiliating, but I also experienced an unexpected freedom. Now that someone else finally knew about my struggle with food, I no longer had to hide it.

Movement away from the counterfeit continues as we learn to recognize and interrupt our addictive cycles. Christopher details his process:

> I spent ten years getting addicted and five years getting sober. I now believe that it takes only a day to get sober or, in fact, a moment. The moment I got sober was when I sat in the anxiety and pain that had become so familiar to me and chose not to act on my desires but rather to open up this infected pocket to the Lord. Rather than shutting Him out, I asked Him to be with me.

I discovered two things in that moment. First, contrary to what my feelings were telling me, I didn't die by not acting out. And second, Jesus Christ met me in the places of my greatest shame. When I heard other people talk about Jesus being enough for them in the face of their temptations, it always sounded so abstract, but in that moment, it was my actual experience.

It took me several more years to own my sobriety on a daily basis. The addiction lost its hold as I began to recognize what triggered me, how I habitually reacted to the triggers, and how they propelled me through an utterly predictable routine. Once my eyes were open to the compulsiveness and self-loathing that were part of the cycle, it became easier to interrupt the cycle, make different choices, and believe in my own worth. Connecting with God and people provided the most effective help. Eventually, the addictive cycle sputtered at stage one—the triggering event—and I knew I was free.

Christopher's experience highlights a crucial component of gaining sobriety: choosing to live in the presence of God at all times. In the sixteen hundreds, a humble Carmelite brother named Lawrence sought to understand how he could remain connected to Jesus and overcome his sin. In several letters to his superiors, Brother Lawrence articulated how he trained his mind to stay present with the Lord:

> Think often of God, day and night, in all your
> tasks, in all your religious duties, even in all your
> amusements. He is always at your side. Do not
> fail in fellowship with him. You would consider it
> discourteous to neglect a friend who visited you.
> Why abandon God and leave him alone? Do not
> then forget him. Think of him often. Worship
> him all the time. Live and die with him. That is
> the Christian's lovely task, in a word, our calling.[14]

We practice living in God's presence by asking Him to stay near even in our moments of temptation and struggle. Although God is never a complicit companion in our sin, He will not abandon us as we surf the web, stop at the massage parlor, or consume an entire bag of chips in one sitting. We practice God's presence when we converse with Him in *each stage of our addictive cycles* until we begin to believe that He really loves us despite ourselves.

As we learn to draw near to Him, we reroute those addictive thought patterns, detach from our counterfeits, and increasingly attach to God and healthy others. Our trust grows. Our confidence deepens. In the course of time, we learn that by pressing into our disappointment and suffering, we discover what we truly desire: to give and receive authentic love. The root of our addictions is not that we have desires; it's that we succumb to our disordered desires and are "too easily pleased."[15]

Our deepening connection with God and our spouses will allow us to restructure our belief systems. Out go the deceptions. No, you don't have to obey your impulses. No, you are not the only Christian woman addicted to pornography. As the lies vaporize, we begin to recognize the extent of our self-deceit and the many ways it has adversely influenced us. These revelations are painful but must be confronted if we are to become more like Christ.

The realignment of our beliefs should not lead us to believe that we are out of the proverbial woods and no longer need to be mindful of our vulnerabilities. In fact, it should have the opposite effect. Some of us will need to disconnect the Wi-Fi and cable in our homes or, at minimum, avoid hypersexualized shows and movies. Others will need to sign up for accountability services,[16] cut up their credit cards, or refrain from ever drinking alcohol. Jesus is our model for resisting temptation. He was tempted in every way that we are, but He did not give in (Heb. 4:15). Regardless of the temptations we face, each of us should make a list of five friends to call when the Evil One hisses, "Did God really say …?"

Scripture promises that God "blesses those who patiently endure testing and temptation" (James 1:12) and that the Lord will show us a way out when we are tempted (1 Cor. 10:13). One safeguard from sin is to proactively "build a complete life with constructive recreation and meaningful work and relationships so the yearnings that so often lead to sin have less of a place in our lives."[17] This will require much of us. But I promise, it's much more satisfying than any of the other options.

Steven's Story

Steven and Cassandra have been married for more than three decades. This brilliant, mega-talented couple reveal Christ's mercy and truth wherever they plant their feet. They courageously offered to share about addiction's impact on their marriage and how God gradually restored them. (Cassandra's story is in chapter 7.)

> **Steven:** I was already sexually addicted when we got married, but I mistakenly thought that marriage would resolve my issues. Cassandra knew some of my struggles, but as most addicts tend to do, I minimized just how pervasive it was. Several years into the marriage, I crossed a line by engaging in risky behavior and knew I had to tell her. Even then, it wasn't the full picture.
>
> At that point, I needed help, so I joined a support group at church, got into therapy, and let my friends know what happened. I made an honest attempt at recovery, but no one really understood what was going on. My therapist didn't even see it as a huge problem, which empowered me to be fooled.

During the next four years, Steven made some progress but failed to understand how habitual masturbation was "fighting the fire with gasoline." The fire heated into an inferno, and one morning Cassandra caught him on the Internet after he had been up all night acting out. This was a pivotal point in their marriage—the proverbial rock bottom. Cassandra was devastated and had to decide if she wanted to stay in the marriage. This time Steven made different choices. He switched to a new therapist—one who recognized the severity of the situation—and joined an accountability group, which he claims saved his life.

> **Steven:** It was wonderful to be in a room with a bunch of honest guys, some of whose lives were falling apart and others who were getting sober. We were all on the same page. I remember the first time I hit thirty days of sobriety. Everyone stood up and clapped for me. It was hugely inspiring.
>
> After nearly twenty years of sobriety, my beliefs about God and myself have shifted. Before, I believed that I was God's exception clause—that God's grace could extend to everyone but me. One of the very real questions I had to wrestle with was *Do I really believe that this God I've been serving all my life can heal me?* I had felt great hopelessness and shame. I wondered if my family and the world would be better off without me. Those questions are settled now.
>
> The settledness and sobriety have had an enormous positive impact on our marriage. Trust

is a lot better than it used to be. I've started to have a correct understanding of sex. I went from believing that sex is everything to seeing that sex is an important part of marriage but certainly not the most important component.

Sobriety does not mean we are never tempted or never fail. It does mean that we recognize our limitations, and rather than skating around the edges of our sin, we hang up the skates. It also means that shame loses its power over us. As the triumphs outweigh the failures, we are no longer controlled by the "psychic malignancy"[18] of addiction.

This is slow and humiliating work, but it is not without measurable rewards. As Christopher and I have found increasing freedom from our disordered attachments and addictions, we are less defensive and more vulnerable. Our trust has deepened, allowing us to attach to each other and God more fully. We have feasted on the bread of life and understand there is no substitute.

Going Deeper

1. When are you tempted to doubt God's promises and His goodness? When are you tempted to doubt your spouse's motivation and love? When doubts or fears surface, how do you respond? Is the connection between doubts, fears, and addictions obvious to you?

2. What behaviors and thought processes do you engage in that cause you to disconnect and create distance from your spouse, God, and others? How does the behavior serve you? (For example, does it prevent you from feeling pain?) How does it harm you?

3. Write down any addictive cycles and explore any broken belief systems that might be embedded in them. (For example, "No one is trustworthy.") Be brutally honest. What are these behaviors and thought patterns costing you and your spouse?

4. Read and meditate on Matthew 4:1–11. Satan offered Jesus counterfeits. How might Jesus's choices inform our choices in similar circumstances?

5. What does it feel like to wait in a posture of faith when you face an unmet need or are being tempted to act out? Name the specific feelings. Now bring that feeling to God and your spouse and see what happens.

7

NONNEGOTIABLES

Confession and Forgiveness

After Christopher ended our first engagement, we didn't speak to each other for two years. Well, that's not totally true. He reluctantly agreed to come to one counseling session with me but was so angry and defensive that dialogue was impossible. He stormed out before the hour ended without even offering to split the fee. During the relational hiatus that followed, we each spent many hours processing what had gone wrong. Prayer helped. Our counselors helped. But we still felt stuck—unable to let go and move on.

One day while I was ostensibly praying but in actuality complaining about this, I sensed God offering me another option. "Fast and pray. For a week." I'm well aware that some people get excited about fasting. I am not one of them. Fasts of any length almost always culminate in headaches, insomnia, and the conviction that I'm wretchedly undisciplined. Nevertheless, my desire to get unstuck trumped all my petty excuses.

About three days into the water fast, I discerned what seemed to be a clear directive from the Holy Spirit: "Confess your bitterness and completely forgive him." There was no promise that obedience would lead to a restored relationship. My response was something along the lines of *Wait. You want me to confess and forgive? What about him? Can we talk about how he broke up with me, for instance?* As if God had forgotten what happened that May morning when the two of us walked along the Charles River. Christopher, creating a clear physical boundary by stuffing his hands in his pockets, communicating in a clinical manner that he needed to break off the engagement and sever all ties with me. Me, in shock and disbelief, begging for an explanation, offering him more time, desperately trying to talk him out of it. *Why do I have to do the work?* I petulantly demanded. The Holy Spirit responded, *Because I'm asking you to.* I started confessing and forgiving that day.

When we incorporate confession and forgiveness into our marriage, we declare our allegiance to the kingdom of God over our allegiance to the kingdom of self. As we admit our sins, we dismantle pride and self-centeredness, two of the most troublesome barriers to transformation. When we choose to forgive, the energy previously allocated for blaming or nurturing anger gets freed up, allowing us to love more wholeheartedly. Obeying God's directive not only purged my bitterness and resentment but also prepared me to reconnect with Christopher and established a precedent that continues to this day. What was true for me is true for all of us: if we want transformed lives and transformed marriages, we need to regularly confess our sins and forgive each other.

Confession: A Primer

Despite the fact that we live in an epoch that tends toward over-sharing, biblical confession remains countercultural. Some years ago, Christopher and I kicked off a retreat with a teaching on this topic. Following the talk, we joined a prayer team around the perimeter of the room and invited folks to confess their sins. One woman made a beeline for me. I assumed that she must have a doozy of a sin to unload. Instead, she somewhat self-consciously admitted that she didn't have anything to confess. I looked at her quizzically and considered asking, "How about denial?" Wisdom prevailed and I prayed a simple blessing over her. Unlike this woman, if I have been awake for more than thirty minutes, I can find something to confess, especially if I've scrolled through my Facebook feed.

Confession is not indiscriminately divulging random thoughts, feelings, and inconsequential mistakes. It's an honest, humble admission of the ways we have fallen short of God's directives and hurt someone—including ourselves—in the process. "Confession acknowledges the need for God and opens the door for God's intervention."[1]

Like the retreat participant, most of us would rather keep the door closed and deny our fallibility. Scripture confronts this tendency. According to the apostle John, whose words are every bit as apropos now as they were two thousand years ago, "If we claim we have no sin, we are only fooling ourselves and not living in the truth" (1 John 1:8). Because the Lord is omniscient, by confessing our sins, we acknowledge what He already knows to be true.

Most of us avoid the jail-worthy sins, such as tax fraud and drug peddling, but silently struggle with the stealthy sins of the heart. We silence those who disagree with us rather than draw them out. We confuse privilege with blessing and blame the have-nots for not having. We gorge when life calls for moderation. No one is going to call 911 on us for such sins, but they are not without cost and should not be omitted from our confessions.

Why Confess?

Why would any of us willingly admit our sins, especially the ones we can hide? We confess because denial thwarts transformation. If we value the appearance of health and wholeness over the real deal, image becomes everything. But if we're serious about wanting to have a dynamic marriage, we have to move through that resistance and become transparent truth tellers.

The Old and New Testaments communicate that God hates lying (Exod. 20:16; Prov. 11:1; Eph. 4:25; Col. 3:9). I wasn't taught this value when I was growing up. Instead, adults routinely demonstrated that lying was acceptable in certain situations. Lies were spoken as a means of protecting my father as he battled his addiction or as a way to avoid conflict. This is why early on in our marriage, I felt no conflict by denying that I was angry when Christopher asked. Regardless of why we choose to dodge the truth, lies are lies. They deaden our consciences, prevent our spouses from knowing us, and provide no impetus to stop sinning.

Confession takes truth telling up a notch. Rather than waiting for our spouses to ask if we finished the bottle of wine, spent several hundred dollars on new clothes, or flirted online, we forthrightly admit it—humbly and nondefensively. It's really quite simple. As James advises, "Confess your sins to each other and pray for each other so that you may be healed" (5:16).

By design, confession mortifies us. We hate having others see our less-than-perfect selves. When we willingly confess our broken thoughts and actions, we allow God to create a crack in the false images that we've worked so hard to perfect. This crack ruins the veneer but also allows forgiveness and grace to seep in.

Years ago while attending a conference out of state, I found myself paying far too much attention to one of the male leaders. Because I felt so embarrassed, I convinced myself that I could manage the crush by myself. Yet after several days of trying to extinguish the feelings, my struggle continued. (I should have simply called Christopher and confessed. I did communicate everything upon my return home.) When it became clear that my efforts were utterly ineffective, I decided to disclose to my small group. Rather than gasp in disbelief and dismiss me as a fraud, they extended forgiveness and prayed for me. Within a few hours, the temptation lifted. Telling the truth did what nothing else could.

Despite that reality, confession continues to be taboo. Until fairly recently, when you stepped into the concourse at Las Vegas Airport, you were greeted with huge banners that read, "What happens in Vegas stays in Vegas." Many well-meaning counselors and talk-show hosts seem to agree with that mind-set. I have a tip for you: don't believe it. Deceit leads to death. Telling the truth leads to healing and life. According to Christopher, men who battle sexually related sins often face internal and external barriers to disclosing their struggles:

> We Christian men often get counsel that says your wife doesn't need to know about your sexual failures because it will only hurt her. Lying is made out to be magnanimity and thoughtfulness. This is self-deceit: a corrupt fellowship in which men wink-wink at the failures of other men rather than holding each other accountable to a godly standard. We need to be unflinching in our definition of sin as well as uncompromising in our application of mercy to those who don't deserve it.

Even if you have a backlog of unconfessed sin, as Steven did, it's never too late. Assuming that your spouse is mature and healthy (meaning that they will not shame or abuse you for telling the truth), ask if your spouse would be willing to hear your confession. When you confess, be specific but spare the gory details. For example, rather than "I spent time on the Internet looking at things that were unhelpful," try "I looked at still images of pornography for three hours this weekend." Specificity helps prevent future sin. We need to own our choices and resist blaming others. Ownership includes apologizing for the ways that our actions or words have affected our spouses.

Christopher and I make a habit to regularly confess the sins and temptations that beg to stay hidden, such as envy, overeating, and cynicism. Unless one of us is planning a surprise party, anything that we're tempted to hide becomes a priority to talk about. If the idea of confession terrifies you, acknowledge that to your spouse and then schedule a time to confess to keep you accountable.

In our marriage, confessions and apologies often happen in that vulnerable space after we've turned off the lights and before we fall asleep. Most nights, I ask the Lord, *How did I do today? Are there any thoughts or actions that I need to confess?* Regardless of how seemingly insignificant they might be, I admit them to Christopher. When I started this practice, I occasionally resisted the Holy Spirit's prompting. It's always easier to rationalize my behavior than humbly and nondefensively say, "I was rude to you at dinner. I'm sorry." This practice keeps my heart soft and serves as an impediment to committing the same sin.

The two of us have been practicing this discipline for the whole of our marriage. If that's not been true for you, please be aware that you might experience turbulence after takeoff. Some confessions will trigger anxiety or anger in your spouse, particularly if the sins you confess directly affect him or her. If you are the only one routinely confessing, you might sometimes wonder if it's worth the humiliation. It is. God will honor your commitment to the truth and bless your faithfulness. The one exception I would make is if your spouse uses your confessions to demean or shame you. In that case, I encourage you to confess to a priest, pastor, or trusted same-gendered friend.

Though confession is not a panacea for all that ails a marriage, I agree with what author Paul David Tripp boldly writes in *What Did You Expect?*: "No change takes place in a marriage that does not begin with confession."[2] When we're truly loved by someone who sees our imperfections and chooses to stand with and love us anyway, it breaks our shame and gives us a taste of God's infinite and redemptive love. This is powerful stuff.

Forgiveness

To follow Christ is to forgive. Once we receive forgiveness vertically from the Lord, we are to give it away horizontally, to our spouses and others. In order to do this well, we need to fully understand what forgiveness is. Sometimes actual events are the best teachers.

In the fall of 2015, a young white man walked into a historic South Carolina church during their midweek Bible study and killed nine African Americans. The family members of the victims publicly expressed their grief but also spoke forgiveness to the murderer. This confounded the secular media, leading some news outlets to view the families' radical choice as denial or insanity.

Forgiveness might seem foolish, but it's certainly not denial. When we drop the charges against those who have sinned against us, we are not excusing their actions, minimizing the damages, or opening ourselves up to further mistreatment. We are simply agreeing that Jesus's redemptive work on the cross is sufficient.

His willingness to die for sins that He did not commit fulfills the ancient laws that preceded His incarnation. When God set the universe in motion, He established physical laws (such as gravity) and spiritual laws (such as the shedding of blood to atone for sin). Prior to Jesus's death on the cross, Hebrew priests heard the confessions of their people and subsequently sacrificed animals so that individuals or tribes could be forgiven. God, who seems slightly detail oriented, specified exactly how these rituals should take place (Lev. 4). For sensitive animal lovers like me, the system seems like a gruesome non sequitur. Yet God deemed that "without the shedding of blood, there is no forgiveness" (Heb. 9:22). The elaborate rituals appeased God but had to be constantly repeated. Jesus's death satisfied the need for sacrifice once and for all. He became our high priest as well as the sacrificial lamb, freeing us from the need to continually shed innocent blood.

This changes everything. Because of Jesus's holy life and sacrificial death, we can "go right into the presence of God"—the Holy of Holies, once reserved for only the high priests—"with sincere hearts fully trusting him. For our guilty consciences have been sprinkled with Christ's blood to make us clean, and our bodies have been washed with pure water" (Heb. 10:22). Today, as we confess our sins to each other and extend forgiveness, we become "a royal priesthood" (1 Peter 2:9 NIV) helping each other inch toward holiness. According to Drs. Paul and Virginia Friesen, "As image bearers of Christ, we are never more Christlike than when we forgive."[3]

The direct causal relationship between confession and forgiveness became apparent to Christopher and me when we reconnected. After that moment when Christopher wondered if he had made a mistake by ending our engagement, he initiated a conversation with me. I was equal parts eager and terrified. When we finally sat down together, it was immediately apparent that we had both changed. In Christopher's words:

I brought no specific expectation to our meeting except that it would be helpful for me to hear what Dorothy's experience had been. Surprisingly, the first thing she said was, "You were right to break up with me," and then confessed her failures. Her ability to completely own her mistakes and forgive me, even though I had not apologized, created a lot of space for me to explore my mistakes without needing to defend myself. This marked an uncharted dynamic in our relationship, and I knew something had changed not only in me but also in her.

As we talked, there was an understandable sadness about how we had hurt each other, but God's presence filled the room. Considering what had transpired between us, it was miraculous that no trace of bitterness existed.

Forgiveness Is a Command, a Choice, and a Process

Our experience during that two-year separation illustrates what we now understand about forgiveness: it's simultaneously a command, choice, and process.

Jesus taught His disciples about the command component on multiple occasions. As recorded by Luke, Jesus said, "If another believer sins, rebuke that person; then if there is repentance, forgive. Even if that person wrongs you seven times a day and each time turns again and asks forgiveness, you must forgive" (Luke 17:3–4). Also quoting Jesus, the apostle Mark writes, "When you are praying, first forgive anyone you are holding a grudge against, so that your Father in heaven will forgive your sins, too" (Mark 11:25).

In certain situations, such as infidelity or habitual deceit, we might be tempted to assume that the command to forgive doesn't apply. Scripture does not validate such spin. When it comes to forgiveness, there are no extenuating circumstances that let us off the hook. (In the case of an abusive spouse, we can forgive while still making choices to protect ourselves and our children. Though we always need to forgive, at times we need to reset boundaries to keep ourselves safe.)[4] If you think your spouse doesn't deserve to be forgiven, you're probably correct. However, those who crucified Jesus didn't deserve to be forgiven either. He forgave them anyway (Luke 23:34).

Like all commands, forgiveness is a choice. God does not coerce or manipulate us; He gives us the terrible freedom to obey—or not. When we obey, God's power gets released into our marriages. And isn't this what we want?

Finally, forgiveness is sometimes a process. As much as we'd like our hurt, bitterness, and anger to completely disappear when we forgive the first time, it's seldom that straightforward. When Peter asked Jesus how many times he was to forgive someone who sinned against him, I can imagine Peter having a little swagger as he suggested seven times. But Jesus countered with "No, not seven times … but seventy times seven!" (Matt. 18:22). That could mean forgiving the same person for the same offense 490 times or that a particular person (who perhaps shares your last name and zip code) sins against you so many times that you have to continually forgive him or her. I am quite confident that in the course of our twenty-five years together, Christopher has needed to forgive me in excess of a thousand times.

Barriers to Forgiveness

We encounter internal and external barriers to forgiving. Consider this example of the latter. You wait thirty, forty, perhaps sixty minutes for a health-care professional. (They have demanding jobs. I'm not intending to be critical.) The person finally walks into the freezing exam room and says, "I'm sorry I kept you waiting." How are you likely to respond? I can almost guarantee that you won't say, "I forgive you." Why? Because social etiquette trains us to play nice and not make others feel guilty, even if that means lying. By verbalizing "I forgive you," we effectively communicate, *Indeed, what you just did cost me something.* It's much easier to dismiss someone's error with a cheery "No problem," even if we're silently fuming. Of course we should be gracious and overlook mistakes, but we should also be aware of the cost of choosing cultural norms over God's ways. Particularly in our marriages, dismissing offenses as no big deal doesn't work long term because no-big-deals tend to morph into very-big-deals.

In order to forgive well and thoroughly, we also have to press through internal barriers. The process of forgiving involves much more than mouthing those three words. Our spouses' sin may arouse a cornucopia of emotions, including anger, pain, betrayal, confusion, and resentment. Although we need to acknowledge rather than deny our feelings, we can't be ruled by them. Christopher and I seldom feel like forgiving each other, and if you watched us after we've had a fight, you might double over in laughter.

Though we've improved over the years, there are still moments when we sit in icy silence immobilized by anger or the desire to be right. Eventually, one of us will grunt something that vaguely resembles an apology. More silence. And then the other will mumble a positively toddler-esque "I forgive you." But—and this is key—once we initiate the process, our hearts always follow. By forgiving, we thwart the Enemy's scheme to divide us.

Apart from our stubborn, willful hearts, perhaps the most significant barrier to forgiving well is our failure to understand the depth of forgiveness that has been extended to us. Author and priest Henri Nouwen explains in *The Road to Daybreak*:

> It is hard for me to forgive someone who has really offended me, especially when it happens more than once....
>
> Maybe the reason it seems hard for me to forgive others is that I do not fully believe that I am a forgiven person. If I could fully accept the truth that I am forgiven and do not have to live in guilt or shame, I would really be free.... A forgiven person forgives.[5]

The more deeply we receive the Lord's forgiveness, the more readily we will be able to extend that same forgiveness to our beloved.

The Consequences of Unforgiveness

Choosing not to forgive has many consequences: first and foremost, we will not be forgiven for our sin. After Jesus responded to Peter's question about how many times he should forgive, Jesus launched into one of the most chilling stories in the New Testament. After a king had generously forgiven a sizable debt from one of his servants, that same servant refused to extend forgiveness to someone who owed him a smaller sum. When the king learned of this, he called in his servant and offered this blistering rebuke:

> "You evil servant! I forgave you that tremendous debt because you pleaded with me. Shouldn't you have mercy on your fellow servant, just as I had mercy on you?" Then the angry king sent the man to prison to be tortured until he had paid his entire debt.
>
> That's what my heavenly Father will do to you if you refuse to forgive your brothers and sisters from your heart. (Matt. 18:32–35)

Is this not one of the most sobering passages in the Bible?

When we withhold forgiveness, it affects us just as significantly as it affects our spouses. We grow bitter and resentful. We tend to magnify their sin, which distorts our perception of who they really are. Finally, studies done by the Mayo Clinic and others have demonstrated that a failure to forgive can result in a host of health problems, such as hypertension, heart issues, depression, anxiety, and a weakened immune system.[6] Though it might feel as though choosing to forgive our spouses costs too much, it's choosing not to forgive that bankrupts us.

Cassandra's Story

A few days after interviewing Steven, I talked with his wife, Cassandra, about her process of forgiving him.

> **Cassandra:** I was not a woman who forgives easily. I was a grudge holder. I guess I was like my own father in this regard. After Steven confessed to me, I was not exactly sure that I wanted to forgive him or even stay married to him. I remember a time when I was lying face-down on the carpet and told God, "I don't really want to be married anymore. I do not feel love for him. If You want me to stay in this marriage, You are going to have to do a miracle, because I'm done."
>
> The miracle was not that I got up from the carpet and had all this love in me. One of the things that shifted was that I began to be on Steven's side. I felt as if I could war against the addiction rather than against him. Gradually,

God put in me a love that was beyond me, beyond what I could muster up. He also put a warrior spirit in me that helped me fight for Steven.

I asked Cassandra how much of that was her effort and how much seemed to be the Holy Spirit's intervention.

Cassandra: There were times when I was simply responding in obedience. It's work to drop the sword. It's work when you feel overwhelmed and feel anger washing over you like a huge wave. I remember when I first found out about his addictions, I thought if I could turn my face to the Light, I could make it through. It was the same thing with letting go of the anger and choosing to forgive: just turn my face.

Visually, it was like a flower, making that slightest turn toward the sun. Maybe heliotropism explains the concept: turning to the Light, who is already there. And in addition, there was photosynthesis. You can't make this happen on your own. All you can do is turn, and God does the rest.

This process of forgiving Steven has totally changed me. I see myself as leather that has been transformed. When you first buy that leather coat, it is stiff and scratchy. This whole process has softened me. As a result, Steven and I enjoy a much deeper intimacy on all levels now. I'm on his side, fighting for him even though I know he's still vulnerable.

From what I know of Cassandra, she is soft and beautiful but simultaneously a warrior for the kingdom. This powerful combination has not only preserved their marriage but also helped countless other men and women who are going through similar battles.

I've often wondered what my life would look like today if I had declined God's invitation to forgive Christopher. I'm not a sentimental person, but this thought causes tears to well up. Without forgiveness, our marriage would not have happened. Our three sons would not exist. We would not have enjoyed twenty-five years of friendship and ministry. In *Forgiving Our Mothers and Fathers*, Leslie Leyland Fields beautifully describes the blessing of forgiveness: "When God freed us from our debts against him, He freed us not to live however we choose, not to pursue our own whims and fancies—but to love more fully."[7] I will never completely understand this mystery, but I know that it's true; forgiveness "leads us to love."[8]

Going Deeper

1. How regularly do you confess sin to your spouse? How long do you tend to wait between the sin and the confession? If you resist confessing, do you know why?

2. How do you respond when your spouse hurts you or sins against you? Where did you learn to respond this way? How effective is your behavior in helping you move toward forgiveness?

3. As you become aware of your broken relational patterns, how would you like to see them change? What kind of support do you need in order for this to happen?

4. After confessing, does your spouse tend to experience lingering guilt or shame? If so, how could you help him or her find more freedom?

5. Do you harbor any unforgiveness toward your spouse? (Unforgiveness sometimes manifests as bitterness, resentment, or disinterest in being intimate. Pay attention to your inner monologue.) Assuming that your marriage is not abusive and your spouse is not currently acting out, if you have resistance to being emotionally or physically intimate, it might be related. What would it take for you to thoroughly forgive him or her?

8

A PARADOX

How Suffering Leads to Love

In an ideal marriage in an ideal world, both the husband and wife contritely admit their faults; never annoy one another, get sick, or lose their jobs; and live happily ever after without ever going through a single crisis. Individual results may vary. Including ours.

My health started to deteriorate during the fall of our ninth year together. For months, a sinus infection stubbornly resisted antibiotics. After it finally cleared, fatigue settled in. I started sleeping ten to twelve hours a night, leading me to wonder if there was a new life growing inside of me. A few weeks later, that was ruled out and a constant, pervasive pain began. It felt as though my body were trapped inside a giant vise that cranked incrementally tighter day after day.

I saw multiple doctors, endured dozens of tests, and then repeated everything with the specialists. We live in Boston, where people come from all over the world for medical treatment, yet no one understood the cause of my rapid decline. A rheumatologist suggested I was depressed and handed me a prescription for an antidepressant. Choking back tears, I responded, "If I'm depressed it's because I am in constant pain and no one is helping me. I'm not sick because I'm depressed—I'm depressed because I'm sick." I tossed the prescription in the trash can as I left.

By that point I was so desperate that I switched medical practices. Soon after, I was finally given the diagnosis of chronic fatigue and fibromyalgia. The subsequent year, celiac disease was added to that list, abruptly ending my bread addiction. Though eliminating gluten reduced some symptoms, my new normal affected almost every aspect of my life. Because of the chronic pain, our intimate life became complicated and compromised. Because I could no longer hold my cameras for more than half a day, my income plummeted. Once fiercely independent, I now needed help doing simple chores, such as raking leaves and changing the bed linens. Fifteen years after the advent of this health crisis, my sons don't remember me as my former self: a robust, athletic woman who bicycled down the West Coast and traveled the world as a journalist.

Throughout the course of our marriages, each one of us will face some type of unexpected crisis. Mine was health related. Christopher's was vocational. Perhaps you have lost a child, have battled mental illness, or have been a victim of a violent crime. When couples vow to love each other despite sickness, extended unemployment, or other unimagined challenges, they don't really know what they're agreeing to. If they did, there might be a long pause between the pastor's question and the couple's response. Because of our one-flesh unions, there's no such thing as an individual crisis. Rather than exempt us from suffering, marriage guarantees that we will suffer.

Though we cannot choose the nature or duration of that suffering, we can choose how we respond. Will we relinquish power and learn to trust God more fully, or will we try to control the circumstances? Will we suffer with Jesus, believing that He is for us (Rom. 8:31), or will we see our crises as evidence of God's disregard? If we can believe that God is for us and ask Him to "make it count"[1] rather than to make it stop, His refining fire will burn off our immaturity and selfishness, allowing our faith to mature. As our faith matures, we begin to understand suffering as purposeful and productive rather than random and meaningless.

After years of chronic health issues, I know this to be true: "We will not be delivered from suffering, but with God's help we can be transformed by it."[2] That transformation includes freedom from regret, a deeper affiliation with Christ, and a greater capacity to love. Truly, this is holy ground.

The Nature of Suffering

Suffering defies a simple, concise definition. It is desperately wanting to stop an addictive behavior but repeatedly failing. It is the unfulfilled longing to be a biological mother. It is being separated from your husband during his yearlong deployment or witnessing your wife's body slowly succumb to cancer.

At its core, suffering is physical or emotional pain or both. Some of the pain we experience in life is foreseeable and therefore slightly more manageable, such as when an aging grandparent dies or when your child moves halfway around the world. Other suffering can never be anticipated and takes our breath away: hearing the words *biopsy, oncologist,* and *surgery* in the same sentence after a routine mammogram; facing corporate downsizing in your fifties; stumbling upon an Internet history that implicates infidelity.

Most of our suffering falls between those two extremes and can often be traced back to our expectations. Perhaps you entered your marriage aware of your spouse's struggle with depression but had no idea how profoundly it would affect you. Perhaps you expected your spouse to gain sobriety from his chemical addiction, but after five years he still struggles. Or maybe you have continued to hope that your wife would receive enough healing from her sexual abuse to enjoy being intimate, only to see that familiar dread in her eyes year after year. Any one of these losses has the potential to escalate into a full-blown crisis.

Suffering affects not only our physical bodies and our human relationships but also our relationship with God. When our bank accounts, bodies, and marriages are healthy, it's easy to proclaim God's faithfulness. If we're in debt, pain, or full-blown marital crises, doubt sometimes causes us to feel ambivalent or even angry with God.

Our Aversion to Suffering

Just as suffering is universal, so is the tendency to avoid it. Describing our aversion to pain, C. S. Lewis writes, "If I knew any way of escape I would crawl through sewers to find it."[3] Some of us do crawl through sewers to avoid suffering. These sewers are more commonly known as affairs, addictions, or any other behaviors that offer a reprieve. Make no mistake: such escapism works if the goal is to *temporarily* avoid suffering. If the goal is to become more like Jesus so that we can love more completely, not so much. Sewer crawling might be an effective diversion, but it detours us away from the vibrant, fulfilling marriages we long to have.

Culture shapes our perspective of suffering. Across the globe, few cultures view suffering through the same lens that Americans do. This is attributable, at least in part, to the influences of secularism and individualism.

Regarding secularism, we prefer to understand ourselves as a Christian nation, but in actuality we are firmly rooted in Enlightenment thinking and Epicurean logic (a system of thought that emphasizes empirical evidence and promotes personal happiness attained by achieving inner peace). Neither of these philosophies are rooted in Christ. In fact, they favor a rational, scientific, Manifest Destiny approach to life that dismisses (or even rejects) the mysterious, spiritual realm in which one believes in and depends upon a sovereign God for life and meaning.

Individualism further distances us from core Christian values. Back in 1830, French political thinker and historian Alexis de Tocqueville observed that "one of the 'novel features' of America was its individualism" and that the American "exists only in himself and for himself alone."[4] As we chase after the elusive goals of personal happiness and self-fulfillment, we make choices that affect our extended families and our communities while seldom allowing their needs or perspectives to influence our choices. Whether it's grad school, a new job, or marriage, we determine what is best for us and then order our lives "according to the narrative of self."[5] Guilty as charged.

From this individual, secular framework, suffering is perceived as little more than a random "evil hiccup"[6] with no redemptive purpose. It becomes an impediment to getting what we want and feeling happy. According to Timothy Keller,

> In the strictly secular view, suffering cannot be a good chapter in your life story—only an interruption of it.… The only thing to do with suffering is to avoid it at all costs, or, if it is unavoidable, manage and minimize the emotions of pain and discomfort as much as possible.[7]

Of course, we can't avoid suffering, and that's one of the problems of pain. Perhaps we can minimize it by trying to remain in control or by cauterizing our hearts. Those options result in a different kind of suffering: profound loneliness. And according to God's plan, loneliness is to be eased by marriage, not exacerbated by it.

The Powerlessness Factor

Suffering reveals our inherent powerlessness. We cannot schedule the delivery date for our pink slips, unilaterally decide to be done with whatever health crises we face, or force our spouses to make better choices.

By minding the moral codes found in Scripture and obeying the laws of the land (e.g., wearing seat belts), we can sidestep *some* suffering. But good behavior does not spare us from all pain and loss. The millions of men, women, and children who have been coerced into slavery worldwide did nothing to deserve it. The righteous and the unrighteous perished alongside one another when the tsunami hit Fukushima, Japan, and when the Twin Towers fell on 9/11. "Suffering dispels the illusion that we have the strength and competence to rule our own lives and save ourselves."[8] It also forces us to confront the erroneous belief that our faith functions as a protective shield.

At some juncture, every one of us will find ourselves in the metaphorical tomb of suffering. When the door slams shut behind us, any illusion that we're in control disappears in the darkness. Shock, disorientation, and claustrophobia close in. We can't make sense of what's happening or make the pain go away. That powerlessness intensifies our suffering.

This was my experience when Christopher unexpectedly ended our relationship and at the onset of my chronic fatigue and fibromyalgia. My friend Jonathan, whom you'll hear from shortly, faced the powerlessness of suffering for three years while hooked up to a kidney dialysis machine. All he could do was wait for an organ donor and pray for God to sustain his life.

How We Respond to Powerlessness and Suffering

Because we're creative people, when we experience powerlessness and suffering, we respond in a myriad of ways.

Fear is often a frequent companion during seasons of suffering. The what-ifs tend to dominate our thoughts and prayers: *What if the chemo doesn't work? What if my spouse is acting out in ways that he hasn't disclosed? What if this marriage never gets easier?* It's as if we're injecting our imagination with toxic steroids, causing it to mutate and self-destruct. If this fear eclipses our view of God, we may succumb to despair.

During the seasons of my most intense suffering, I've had moments of despair that incapacitated me. This was in part because "I felt like my right now was my new forever."[9] I believed tonight's crazy-making insomnia would never lift or that I would always feel this angry with Christopher. When we project our current suffering onto tomorrow, we can easily assume that God will never intervene, because He doesn't seem to be intervening now.

One of the ways we try to avoid powerlessness and the accompanying despair is by blaming others. Stephen Sondheim's brilliant play *Into the Woods* includes a song called "Your Fault." In it, the characters pass the blame for the devastating circumstances that have befallen their community onto others rather than admitting their shared culpability. How like us. When we're in a difficult place, it's much easier to attribute our troubles to others than for us to accept responsibility.

In our worst moments, we sometimes even blame God for our misfortunes. We cannot make sense of the apparent contradiction that an all-loving, all-powerful God would not protect us from pain and loss. We often demand answers and then make false conclusions about our Father if those answers never come. When we pummel God with *why* questions, we don't want a theological explanation; we want to lodge an official complaint about the unfairness of the situation as well as God's seeming indifference.

Anger often follows close on the heels of blame. Sometimes anger seems to be the only leverage we have in the face of powerlessness. We get angry with and berate ourselves if personal choices contribute to our current situations: *Why did I ignore those health symptoms for so long?* We get angry with our spouses: *Why did you ignore those health symptoms for so long?* And we even get angry with God: *Since You created the earth, would it be too much to ask You to heal my body?* Although railing at others might temporarily alleviate some of the tension, if we get stuck in a cycle of anger and blame, it will not only prolong and exacerbate our suffering but also lead to regret.

Regret is a more internal, passive response to suffering. The year 2013 was filled with regret for Christopher and me. As soon as it became clear that God was asking us to leave our beloved church community, Christopher tendered his resignation, and immediately our battle with regret began. On an almost nightly basis, we revisited cues that we apparently missed, replayed conversations that had long since ended, and reevaluated decisions we had already made. There was no next job lined up and no suggested six months of savings. Our bills did not magically cease, a reality that occasionally looped us back into our little regret binges.

"Regret is never, ever meant to be a destination,"[10] writes Michelle Van Loon in *If Only: Letting Go of Regret.* But for most of us, regret becomes a way of life. We regret the sarcastic retorts we give our spouses, but we don't do the hard work of making sure that behavior does not continue. We regret opening that website but don't disclose our struggle to anyone. Regret can become "a form of self-punishment,"[11] a way for us to save face and avoid repenting. Regret tricks us into believing that if we work at something long enough, we will be able to create an alternate universe where everything comes out perfect, à la Bill Murray in *Groundhog Day.* Meanwhile, as the sun continues to rise and set on the rest of humanity, we remain stuck. After all, retakes only happen in Hollywood.

Denial and avoidance are other methods of coping with pain and suffering. They can take many forms, such as putting in excessively long hours at work; overinvesting in our children, pets, and hobbies; or opting for virtual relationships. Denial and avoidance redirect our focus away from the perceived source of our pain to something that provides pleasure or demands less of us. Although our desire to dodge pain and powerlessness is understandable, such choices will prohibit us from experiencing suffering's redemptive purposes.

Finding God and His Purposes in Our Suffering

When we're in the tomb of suffering, our default behavior tends to be either frantically clawing the walls to create a way out or numbing ourselves so we forget where we are. We have other options. Though the pain disorients and confuses us, if we wait for our eyes to adjust and then look for Jesus Christ, we make surprising discoveries.

First, we discern that we are not alone. Scripture promises us that God will never leave us (Heb. 13:5). Even when we walk through the darkest valley, He is close beside us, protecting and comforting us (Ps. 23:4). On those days when we feel certain our marriages will not survive or when unrelenting physical pain mocks us, we need not fear that our Savior has abandoned us. How do we dare trust His prodigal love? As Ann Voskamp points out, He has already proven Himself faithful:

> If trust must be earned, hasn't God unequivocally earned our trust with the bark on the raw

> wounds, the thorns pressed into the brow, your
> name on the cracked lips? How will He not also
> graciously give us all things He deems best and
> right? He's already given the incomprehensible.
>
> Christ our Crossbeam.[12]

Second, though suffering often appears arbitrary, it need not be meaningless. God's priorities for us don't always coincide with our priorities. We want happy marriages. He wants us to have marriages characterized by joy that is not dependent upon what our spouses do or don't do. We want effortless marriages. He calls us to another broken human being who will force us to our knees in fervent prayer. Hebrews 10:10 helps us understand the bigger picture: "God's will was for us to be made holy by the sacrifice of the body of Jesus Christ, once for all time." God wants this for us not because He is a cruel despot but because He longs for us to be like His crucified Son, who loved perfectly and sacrificed to the point of death.

We often exert a tremendous amount of energy trying to get God to change our circumstances. He uses the circumstances to change us. For us to come around to God's perspective, we have to submit our wills and our desires to Him. In *A Beautiful Disaster*, author Marlena Graves explains His objectives:

> In the wilderness, we remember that God did not
> bring us out here in the desert to die. He brought
> us out here to save us, to show us his power, to
> offer his comfort, and to put to death whatever is
> in us that is not of him.[13]

Jesus shows us how to submit in faith. Just before his betrayal, He prayed in the garden, "Father, if you are willing, please take this cup of suffering away from me. Yet *I want your will* to be done, not mine" (Luke 22:42).

If we come to understand pain as God's megaphone[14] to rouse us from our self-induced comas, we can experience suffering as a divine mercy. It forces us to face ugly realities, such as the fact that selfishness comes more naturally than sacrificial love or that we prefer the ease of sameness over the challenges of sacred otherness. Particularly in the context of marriage, nothing excavates the hardened soil of our hearts like suffering.

The entire arc of Scripture reveals the transformative power of pain and suffering. Because we live in a culture that prefers sentimentality to reality, we tend to reduce biblical narratives to Disney-style movies and thus miss their profoundly applicable messages. (No offense to those of you who self-identify as Disney fans, but they typically soften the edges and occasionally veer off script.)

Consider Joseph. After he told his brothers about a series of prophetic dreams that inflamed their jealousy and resentment, they betrayed him by selling him as a slave. He was separated from his family for approximately twenty years. Joseph suffered many other injustices, including being wrongly accused by Potiphar's wife and serving jail time. We don't have an account telling us how he navigated those two decades. Did he doubt whether his dreams were indeed from God? Did he despair of ever being free or seeing his family again?

We do know that Joseph experienced God's presence and His favor during this time. Even Potiphar realized that "the

LORD was with Joseph, giving him success in everything he did"
(Gen. 39:3). God's favor did not result in Joseph's sentence being
commuted. Reading between the verses, it seems that Joseph
surrendered to his circumstances while holding on to the reality
that God was with him and for him. This allowed Joseph to live
unto the Lord without fear.

Submitting in the midst of suffering requires supernatural
faith. Hebrews 11:1 reads, "Faith shows the reality of what we
hope for; it is the evidence of things we cannot see." The fear
that creeps in while we suffer exposes our struggle to believe in
God's goodness and provision. It's all too easy to forecast our
futures based on our current pain and rightly predict our insuf-
ficiency. We fail to take into account that faith is like manna:
we cannot store it up for tomorrow. God provides only what we
need for each day.

Back to Joseph. At the beginning of the narrative, he was
an arrogant, prideful teen with little regard for his siblings.
Eventually, his brothers dramatically fulfilled his dream. Mid-
famine, the desperate clan walked from Canaan to Egypt,
arrived before Joseph (but failed to recognize him), and "bowed
before him with their faces to the ground" (Gen. 42:6). After
many plot twists and much intrigue, Joseph revealed himself to
his family:

> Then Joseph could no longer control himself
> before all his attendants, and he cried out,
> "Have everyone leave my presence!" So there
> was no one with Joseph when he made himself

known to his brothers. And he wept so loudly
that the Egyptians heard him, and Pharaoh's
household heard about it. (Gen. 45:1–2 NIV)

This was his denouement, and I don't think it unfolded
according to his earlier script. He does not gloat by saying, "Hey,
remember that dream I had, the one that made you all so angry?
Isn't it funny how this played out?" Instead, Joseph nearly collapses
under the weight of his grief and loss. He is not the same egotisti-
cal youth who was sold into slavery two decades earlier. Suffering
had completed its work in him. Now full of wisdom, empathy, and
understanding, he assures them with one of most oft-quoted verses
in the Bible: "You intended to harm me, but God intended it all
for good. He brought me to this position so I could save the lives
of many people" (Gen. 50:20).

Rather than succumb to unbelief and bitterness, do I dare
believe that my suffering has the capacity to save my spouse's life?
Not in a messianic fashion but by making me enough like Jesus
that I can love him when he feels unlovable, forgive him when
he feels unforgivable, or touch him when he feels untouchable. If
you feel consumed by feelings of meaninglessness try praying, *God,
reveal yourself to me and don't let me waste this pain.*

Holding Each Other Up

God does not intend for us to fight battles or suffer alone. In Eve,
Yahweh gave Adam a warrior companion, an *ezer*,[15] who would
stand by that same scarred side from which she was taken, to

govern and rule the earth with him (Gen. 1:26–28). Whether or not we realize it, when we say our vows, we are promising to ease each other's aloneness, particularly when things aren't going well. Exodus 17 gives us a vision for what this might look like.

The Israelites were in the midst of a battle and could advance against the Amalekites only when Moses held his staff above his head. A peculiar strategy, but God seems to relish supernatural displays of power that mankind cannot take credit for. Inevitably, "Moses' arms soon became so tired he could no longer hold them up. So Aaron and Hur found a stone for him to sit on. Then they stood on each side of Moses, holding up his hands. So his hands held steady until sunset. As a result, Joshua overwhelmed the army of Amalek in battle" (Exod. 17:12–13).

What if we decide to be like Aaron and Hur to our spouses? What if we come alongside them, hold up their arms when their strength starts to fail, and refuse to leave until the battle is done? By making this choice, we will emerge from our seasons of suffering as healed and holy lovers. Bone of my bone. Flesh of my flesh.

Jonathan and Talisa's Story

Jonathan and Talisa are two of the most passionate followers of Christ that Christopher and I have ever met. For the past ten years, they have been living and ministering in South Africa. I asked them to share how suffering has changed them and, consequently, their marriage.

Talisa: The two seasons of suffering that come to mind are when I had a miscarriage and when Jonathan was on kidney dialysis. After the miscarriage, I wanted him to be a different man. I was in such turmoil, really confused about what happened and why it happened. I wanted to be comforted. I wanted to pray and process. What I got was his being cut off. There was no expressed emotion. It was a hopeless place for me. I knew I couldn't change him, so I packed away my needs and emotions.

Jonathan: I'm the person who doesn't feel anything immediately. I need to process intellectually before I can access my feelings. When we lost our child, there was no point of reference. I knew something bad had happened but wasn't sure what I was supposed to feel. I was a blank slate. I felt helpless but just put my head down and kept going.

This is not completely different from how I handled it when my father died. I was nineteen. As a young black man in a white context, I was taught to always be in control of my emotions because people who were in control would not let anything affect them. I learned to intimidate people and protect myself with my intelligence rather than my emotions.

Talisa: There was a double layer of suffering: for the lost child and also for the reality that Jonathan could not be who I wanted or needed him to be. We go into marriage not really knowing who the other person is. I had a reality check. *This is who you really are?* I knew I was going to persevere in this but did not know how it was going to turn out.

Jonathan: I don't trust my negative emotions with others, and that includes God. When my father died, I was angry at him and God. But I did not allow myself to feel the anger and grief because I thought, *You don't have the right to bring your questions to God. How dare you!* In the midst of my kidneys shutting down and having to be on dialysis for twelve to sixteen hours a week, I would think, *It could be worse.* What this reflected was my inability to trust God with my emotions. I made a false peace with my disappointment and called it contentment.

When I was doing a ministry training in South Africa, God broke through my tendency to become a Vulcan in the face of pain. [Vulcans were characters in *Star Trek* who were intellectual but emotionally cut off.] I was in a room with five white Afrikaners, still trying to hold it all together, maybe more so because in a racial context, these men represented the enemy. In the midst of this, the Holy Spirit communicated to me, *You've been holding on to stuff for years, and it's to the point where either you will die or someone else will. These are the people I have chosen to accompany you in your healing.* And then I broke.

Our suffering has deeply affected us. I'm now more vulnerable before the Lord and also with Talisa and our children. Because of what we have been through, we are both more alert to how we respond emotionally. We make it a point to check in with each other about everything. It has also shaped our awareness and willingness to help others process their suffering.

Like Steven and Cassandra, Jonathan and Talisa have allowed Jesus to change them through their suffering. Rather than becoming bitter or indulging in self-pity, they have said yes to Jesus. In the process, they have been transformed into powerful conduits for the Lord's healing power. It's no exaggeration to write that people across the globe have been, and will continue to be, influenced by their lives.

Writers who are more mature than I am would close this chapter by confirming that they would never trade their losses for what they've gained through suffering. I agree with the sentiment, but if the Lord had asked me to weigh in, I would have written my story differently. I'd prefer to eat whatever I want and live without chronic pain. But because God doesn't hire ghostwriters, my choices are limited to how I respond in the face of my suffering and loss.

In the moments when I feel discouraged or weary, I return to Lewis's words in *The Problem of Pain*:

> We are, not metaphorically but in very truth, a Divine work of art, something that God is making, and therefore something with which He will not be satisfied until it has a certain character....
>
> To ask that God's love should be content with us as we are is to ask that God should cease to be God: because He is what He is, His love must, in the nature of things, be impeded and repelled by certain stains in our present character, and because He already loves us He must labour to make us lovable.[16]

This perspective challenges me not to waste my suffering but rather to let it complete God's work in me so that I can faithfully and radically love. When I submit to His story, He does not abandon me in the valley of loss and sorrow but ultimately leads me to a place of abundance and joy. I am forever grateful.

Going Deeper

1. What is your default response to suffering? What is your spouse's default? Do you run toward or away from God? Do you move toward or away from your spouse?

2. How do you respond to your spouse when he or she is suffering? Can you readily and consistently offer comfort and stay emotionally present to his or her needs? If not, why? Are there any situations in which your spouse has grown weary and might need you to hold up his or her arms as Aaron and Hur did for Moses?

3. How has suffering changed you? Is there room to grow? If so, how?

4. In your seasons of suffering, has God felt near or absent? Consider how your mother and father responded to you when you were suffering. Is there any thematic overlap? If so, explore any unhealed wounds from your family of origin that might make it difficult for you to access God.

5. How do you feel about the possibility that suffering will play a role in helping you become the kind of husband or wife you long to be? Discuss this with your spouse.

9

CHOOSING JOY

God's Secret Weapon

Our eldest son got married before he could legally buy champagne to celebrate. He met his future wife the first month of college, and within a year it was obvious that their relationship was headed to the altar. Because Christopher and I were significantly older when we married (twenty-seven and thirty, respectively), we had no frame of reference for this. Should we insist they wait or come alongside them and bless their choice? After many discussions and much prayer, we chose the latter. There's never been a moment of doubt.

To be more specific, there's never been any doubt about the two of them choosing to spend their lives together. In the weeks leading up to the event, Christopher and I had lots of doubts, such as whether or not we would make it to the wedding day with our mental health intact. Those of you who have planned and pulled off a major event know that the normal demands of life don't suddenly cease despite the ever-expanding to-do lists. And in our case, there were some extenuating circumstances that further tapped our reserves: three family members (including my father) were battling cancer, and multiple friends questioned our wisdom in allowing our son to get married before finishing college.

Then there were the unique challenges that Christopher and I brought to the table. You have probably discerned from the previous chapters that we are rather opinionated individuals. We're also creative and frugal. Being opinionated, frugal, *and* creative is a dangerous combination when it comes to buying a house or planning a wedding. We wanted the two of them to have a beautiful, elegant day but had limited resources to contribute. When they finally found a venue that met everyone's criteria for beauty and elegance, not surprisingly, it exceeded both families' budgets.

Given all the factors (and our general state of delirium), we decided to host the reception at our house. At this reception, not only did we want locally sourced food but it had to be free of gluten, dairy, and high-fructose corn syrup—and under ten dollars a head. Did I mention that Christopher and I were officiating the ceremony? At least I had enough wisdom to hire a photographer rather than assume I could handle that too.

As the date approached, it became obvious to Christopher and me that we had a choice to make. Were we going to allow the details, the pressure, the naysayers, and the shrinking checking account to consume us, or were we going to choose joy? This was not a onetime decision that we could smartly pivot on but rather a gradual turning toward the extravagant God who loves to bless His children. We said yes to Him.

Joy saturated the wedding day. With the exception of the naked Bacchus statue that stood directly behind us, the ceremony was perfect. We recalled God's faithfulness and worshipped Him. We laughed and we cried. Under a huge tent in our front yard, sunflowers and zinnias adorned the festive tables that were heavy laden with succulent barbecue and all the trimmings. Several hours later when the happy couple drove off for their honeymoon, we were filled with gratitude that God had brought them together and given them sufficient courage to pledge their lives to each other. My only regret was that we did not put the house on the market the next day, as it will never look that good again.

The joy that we experienced helped Christopher and me realize that during the years leading up to the wedding, we had morphed into Eeyore. Though the two of us have always been intense, we've also known how to laugh and enjoy life. Somehow our departure from the church we loved and the sudden death of Christopher's mother from pancreatic cancer (which happened concurrently) had stolen our joy. It was time to take it back.

As we fought for joy, we discovered something: the joy of the Lord is one of the most dynamic forces available to us. It has the power to turn our mourning into dancing, our despair into hope, and our fear into faith. This joy is a by-product of our transformation as well as an essential component of the process. Regardless of your temperament or your circumstances, rest in this truth: God intends for all of us to experience His abundant joy.

Defining Joy

Joy functions like engine oil. It reduces relational friction, which not only helps us uphold our commitment to each other but also rejoice in it. Joy runs deeper than happiness because it has the capacity to transcend the details of our lives. Author and speaker Margaret Feinberg explains in *Fight Back with Joy*, "The Bible insists that joy is more than a feeling; it's an action. We don't just sense joy; we embody it by how we respond to the circumstances before us."[1]

As Feinberg points out, one example of God's people choosing joy in the face of challenging circumstances can be found in the book of Nehemiah.[2] After the wall around Jerusalem had been rebuilt under Nehemiah's leadership (approximately 450 BC), the Israelites returned to the city and assembled in the square around the Water Gate. For the most part, they had not been obeying the Mosaic law. When their priest, Ezra, read God's Word to them, they were deeply convicted and wept. Nehemiah responded to their grief in a surprising fashion:

> Don't mourn or weep on such a day as this! For today is a sacred day before the LORD your God....
>
> Go and celebrate with a feast of rich foods and sweet drinks, and share gifts of food with people who have nothing prepared. This is a sacred day before our Lord. Don't be dejected and sad, for the joy of the LORD is your strength! (Neh. 8:9–10)

This passage and many others seem to indicate that joy emanates from God. Joy is not a saccharine, sentimental emotion, nor is it a facade. It is a mighty river that flows from the headwaters of God's fierce love for us.

Feinberg, who was fighting an aggressive form of cancer as she wrote *Fight Back with Joy*, continues,

> The tigerish love of God from which joy comes is foundational to faith. God's love guards us, protects us, grows us, strengthens us, and compels us to walk in greater trust and holiness. This is no passive affection, but a feisty, fiery pledge to grow us into the fullness of Christ. When we embrace this love and cultivate an awareness of it, our hearts are filled with joy.[3]

Based on verses such as "Restore to me the joy of your salvation" (Ps. 51:12) and "I will be filled with joy because of you" (9:2), it seems that as with our salvation, we don't initiate joy; rather, we respond to the Lord's initiative. Provided that we remain in relationship with Him, the flow of His joy will not be dammed up or diverted (19:8).

Our awareness and experience of God's miraculous saving grace leads us deeper into joy. In his letter to the Romans, Paul declares,

> Oh, what joy for those
> > whose disobedience is forgiven,
> > whose sins are put out of sight.
> Yes, what joy for those
> > whose record the LORD has cleared of sin.
> > > (Rom. 4:7–8)

Conversely, walking in sin or failing to confess sin seems to block God's joy. King David's raw words revealed his emotional state as a result of his unconfessed sin:

> When I refused to confess my sin,
> > my body wasted away,
> > and I groaned all day long.
> Day and night your hand of discipline was
> > heavy on me.
> My strength evaporated like water in the
> > summer heat. (Ps. 32:3–4)

Joy does not swallow up our grief or mourning. In fact, it seems that the ability to experience joy is directly related to the ability to feel pain. Author Jerry Sittser observes that "the soul is elastic, like a balloon. It can grow larger through suffering.... Once enlarged, the soul is also capable of experiencing greater joy, strength, peace, and love."[4] Feinberg elaborates, "When we don't allow ourselves to grieve well, something inside us dies. Our bandwidth for feeling narrows and emotional signals seem to fade. We may not feel as much pain, but we also don't feel as much joy."[5] It's been my experience that those who try to distance themselves from pain and suffering are also the ones whose happiness seems unconvincing and one-dimensional.

Shifting the Paradigm

The apostles and early believers understood the connection between joy and suffering. I cannot fathom how they endured such persecution, let alone chose joy. They were imprisoned, beaten, hideously tortured, and often killed, simply because they followed Jesus. James encouraged young Christians by writing, "Consider it pure joy, my brothers and sisters, whenever you face trials of many kinds, because you know that the testing of your faith produces perseverance. Let perseverance finish its work so that you may be mature and complete, not lacking anything" (1:2–4 NIV).

For years, I bristled when reading this verse. I felt as though I was being forced to swallow a tincture of denial. And, furthermore, it wasn't perseverance that I wanted. I wanted circumstances to change: for my health to improve, for our income to increase, and for Christopher to come home on time. After all, is it even fair for the Lord to ask us to stand in joy in the midst of life's trials?

This isn't an issue of fairness; it's an issue of obedience. When we choose joy in the midst of our suffering, we defiantly proclaim that death and destruction will not have the final word—we're choosing to trust God even though we may not understand how things will play out.

The Bigger Picture

In order to choose joy and prevent death and destruction from defining us, we simply need to stay connected to the source and keep our hearts responsive. Easy, right? Not so much. It demands tremendous intentionality and resolve to cleave to God and keep our wounded hearts responsive to Him, not because God is untrustworthy, but because we're in a great battle with a formidable Enemy.

This Enemy is not content to occasionally lob a few smoke bombs in our direction and then retreat. Satan and his demons continuously assault us from every angle, with every possible weapon. Their primary tactic is to turn us against God by maligning Him, which leads us to doubt His love for us. If we give in to that doubt, we lose our joy and our peace.

On a day-to-day basis, we try to distance ourselves from the unseen realm (see Eph. 6:12) because spiritual warfare offends our postmodern sensibilities. We find it easier to believe that our spouses are hopelessly dim-witted rather than attribute our frustration to the thief who wants to steal, kill, and destroy (see John 10:10). It's imprudent to assume there's a demon inspiring every moment of marital friction, but it's also foolhardy to ignore the larger spiritual reality.

Satan is a master of spin and an unapologetic opportunist. While we're arguing and blaming each other, we lose track that the Enemy wants nothing more than to keep us in the trenches and ultimately destroy our marriages. Why does he care whether our marriages succeed or fail? Because when a man and a woman sacrificially love each other, they reveal the image of God to the world—and Satan detests this.

Based on our personal and pastoral experience, it seems that the healthier the marriage, the more it's opposed. Conversely, once a husband and wife are routinely bickering, withholding affection, and refusing to forgive each other, the Enemy has completed his assignment and can move down the road to the next household. It's when we dismantle the walls that divide us and refuse to put them back up that he notices.

Scripture is one of our primary weapons in this war. God's truth counters the Enemy's lies by offering us a narrative of His goodness, faithfulness, and love. As demonstrated by the manna given to the wandering Israelites (Exod. 16) and the Bread of Life offered to all of us, we have a Father in heaven who provides for our needs. Do we dare believe that the same God who casts out demons, heals the sick, and triumphs over death will also give us whatever we need to create and sustain healthy marriages? In my experience, He does this and so much more.

If we're going to emerge victorious in this battle, we have to discern when we're under attack. Obvious indicators of enemy activity include ongoing strife (as detailed in chapters 2 through 4) and fear. Throughout Scripture, God acknowledges our tendency to fear and then admonishes us not to give in to it. That's why the angel Gabriel told Mary, "Don't be afraid" even before he invited her to be part of God's audacious plan (Luke 1:30). That's why as Moses was handing over the reins of leadership to Joshua he said, "Do not be afraid or discouraged, for the LORD will personally go ahead of you. He will be with you; he will neither fail you nor abandon you" (Deut. 31:8).

As I mentioned earlier, Christopher and I continue to battle fear. It primarily manifests as worrying, awfulizing, and occasional bizarre behavior. Christopher's anxiety about someone breaking into our first urban apartment led him to sprinkle baby powder all over the back stairs. It was hardly irrefutable logic. If someone had broken in, at least we would have been able to identify their shoes. When the boys were younger, we worried that some terrible sickness would consume their fragile bodies. Now in our fifties, we obsessively scan our skin for irregular moles and wonder if our forgetfulness is simply part of the aging process or evidence of dementia. In *Anxious*, author Amy Simpson articulates these fears:

> Worry tends to consume us....
>
> It often acts ... like tar, keeping us stuck in indecision and even emotional or mental paralysis....
>
> Worry reinforces the idea that everything is up to us. That idea causes more worry, which fuels a false sense of responsibility, which gives birth to a gigantic desire for control.[6]

In the Sermon on the Mount, Jesus addresses our propensity to worry:

> That is why I tell you not to worry about everyday life—whether you have enough food and drink, or enough clothes to wear.... Can all your worries add a single moment to your life? ...
>
> Seek the Kingdom of God above all else, and live righteously, and he will give you everything you need.
>
> So don't worry about tomorrow, for tomorrow will bring its own worries. Today's trouble is enough for today. (Matt. 6:25, 27, 33–34)

Installing security systems, stashing valuables in safe-deposit boxes, or storing a year's supply of dehydrated food in the basement might seem judicious, but none of these strategies resolve the bigger issue: can we trust God *with everything*? In fact, is it possible that such activistic behavior causes our fears to grow because it leads us to believe that we have more power than we actually do? We win the battle over fear through confessing, aligning our thoughts to the truth in Scripture, and choosing to live as if God really is in control. God's joy helps us succeed in each of those endeavors.

Fighting for Joy

Maybe I was withholding a key detail when I wrote that joy is a gift from God. Receiving a gift implies opening up our hands and accepting what's being offered. Living in joy requires something from us: we must push back against the darkness through worship, gratitude, and prayer.

Fighting for Joy through Worship

One of Christopher's main gifts is leading worship. This entails far more than having a powerful voice and being an expressive pianist, both of which are true of him. He understands that proclaiming God's goodness in the face of uncertainty and ongoing losses refutes the Enemy's constant assault on God's character. Christopher shares his experience of the worship-joy connection:

Any worship leader worth his or her salt leads a congregation of one. Redirecting the self toward God and genuine faith is far more difficult than leading the band and the vocalists. To lead others in worship, I have to take authority over my own soul first and foremost, and the most effective way for me to do that is to sing. Psalm 103 says, "Bless the Lord, O my soul, and forget not all His benefits" (KJV). The psalmist was telling himself to praise God. It was an act of his will. What surprises me again and again is how choosing to engage and declaring God's goodness through song refreshes my soul and empowers me to live in the fullness of God's calling.

To worship means to submit one's voice, mind, and body to the Truth. Worship involves speaking and singing but also physicalizing praise. It's not enough to just think about God. We're flesh and blood. Therefore, our earthly worship has to involve all of who we are. Paul expanded the definition of worship in his letter to the Romans:

> Dear brothers and sisters, I plead with you to give your bodies to God because of all he has done for you. Let them be a living and holy sacrifice—the kind he will find acceptable. This is truly the way to worship him. (12:1)

We can do this whether we're kneeling in a cathedral, walking through the woods, or sitting in our living room. We can do it in seasons when we feel near to God or when we cannot sense His presence. Because Christopher and I know that we cannot rely on Sunday morning service to meet all of our needs, we regularly invite friends over to worship and pray. Sometimes there are babies cooing and crying. Our irreverent dog often rolls around in the middle of the floor. These gatherings solidify our faith, strengthen us for the battles, and create a unified front. They are always among the highlights of my year.

Fighting for Joy through Gratitude

Worship is intimately connected to gratitude. Like worship, gratitude is not an automatic human response. We have to train ourselves to have grateful hearts. Perhaps it's endemic to our culture or maybe it's human nature, but we always seem to want more. As the authors of *Slow Church* observe, "What is absent can obscure what is present."[7] To choose gratitude is to reject the greed and entitlement that pervades our day. This has been an ongoing struggle for me.

Throughout our marriage, Christopher has encouraged me to get away once a year. I typically drive to a friend's cottage and spend several days reading, walking along the beach, and praying. It always restores my soul and resources me to reengage with life. If I return from my mini-sabbatical and discover that the dishes have piled up, the laundry has not been done, and the dog has vomited in a remote corner (and strangely, no one else has noticed), I have a choice to make. Will I become indignant and express my disappointment? Or will I hug Christopher and express my gratitude? When I choose poorly, the benefits of my time away instantly vanish.

If we can discipline ourselves to choose gratitude over complaining and fault-finding, not only will our spiritual lives improve but so will our marriages. The depth of our gratitude is directly connected to our ability to trust in God's love and remember His faithfulness. Because God understands the human tendency to forget, He commanded the Israelites to set aside seven times a year to recall His faithfulness. This includes Passover, when God spared His people from the angel of death, and Purim, when Queen Esther's courageous actions prevented genocide.

Because most Christian traditions lack holy days specifically for giving thanks, we have to be intentional about expressing our gratitude. Consider incorporating thanksgiving into communion or carving out some time for the sole purpose of expressing gratitude. One afternoon, a friend and I committed to thank God for any and every gift we could call to mind. Our impromptu praise went on for almost two hours.

Gratitude shifts our perspective off the mundane—the dishes, the diapers, the crushing disappointment—and onto the reality that we have life and breath and a God who saves. Though I'm aware of this transcendent reality, I struggle to consistently stay in a posture of gratitude. Gratitude requires effort. Complaining seems effortless. Before I'm fully awake, I can grumble to the Lord about my frustrations regarding my lack of sleep, my aching body, and the annoying songbird that starts her day at oh-dark-thirty.

Or, option B, I can wake up and praise God that even though I can no longer run or bike, I can still walk. I can thank Him that even though I can't eat real bread or pizza, I can still eat chocolate. I can thank Christopher for going to work every day and giving me the space to write this book rather than insisting that I get a real job. As I have been making an effort to choose option B, I've discovered that gratitude allows me to stay connected to God, purges entitlement, and opens me up to possibilities rather than causing me to tunnel in on my losses.

Fighting for Joy through Prayer

Like worship and gratitude, prayer moves us toward God, changing us and our perspective in the process. Regardless of what we're hoping for, when we begin praying, we typically want God to change our circumstances. Sometimes He answers our prayers along the lines of our requests. But even if God chooses not to solve our problems the way we imagine, prayer changes us. It is through prayer that we experience the slow conversion of our worldly desires to the transcendent will of God. Jen Pollock Michel describes this:

> Whatever prayer is, it is real participation with God....

> Prayer, in fact, is never only about getting what we want from God. It is a bold invitation to meet with God in our authentic human experience, which is to say doubt and desire, praise and perplexity, fear and failure.[8]

When we pray together as husband and wife, we not only solidify our defenses against the Enemy's attack but also experience a level of closeness that is rivaled only by sexual intimacy. When too many days have passed since our last time of praying together, I am hungry to approach the Lord with Christopher. Whether it's for five minutes or twenty-five minutes, it's always a joyful exclamation point to our day.

Ryan and Natasha's Story

Natasha and Ryan embody the joy of the Lord. That joy spills over into every aspect of their lives, including their marriage, parenting, and leadership. I started the interview by asking them to define joy.

> **Natasha:** It's deeper than happiness but includes happiness. It means I have overflowing love for others. It means I have a greater potential to love and to see the good in a situation.

Ryan: It's having an overreaching capacity—having more capacity than I know I have by myself.

Natasha: And it's contagious. When I'm with my best friend, we lift each other through our joy. Then I bring it back to our home. It's almost as if I'm a vessel, as I did not create what I'm carrying.

Ryan: We bring this joy into our marriage when we keep one another from taking ourselves too seriously. Natasha has a tendency to worry and think about worst-case scenarios. I make light of this by referring to her as Worst-Case-Scenario Girl and sing her the chorus of an original theme song I wrote that helps her lighten up.

Natasha: Ryan makes me laugh all the time. He sent me a text this morning that had me laughing out loud in the grocery store. Sex also brings us a lot of joy. Intimacy is not performance oriented; it's playful and honoring. We sense the joy of the Lord when we're together.

As an example of their playfulness, when I asked them to talk about the role of worship as it connects to joy, Natasha started to respond by saying, "My husband is really talented …" Before she could finish the sentence, Ryan interjected, "Is that comment about sex? Because if it is, I want that line in the book."

Natasha laughed, answered affirmatively, and then clarified, "He's a really talented musician. When he's playing the guitar and singing, I'll join him. We're worshipping the Lord, but there's something more happening. My voice is a spiritual turbine that helps his worship go deeper and encourages him. We're very unified in these moments."

> **Ryan:** We worship together at least twice a week, sometimes with the kids but not always. Worship does not feel like something that we do and then stop doing. It flows. It's worked into the routine of our lives at this point.

God's joy has helped them through some difficult seasons in their marriage, such as Natasha's bumpy adjustment to mothering and Ryan's loss of his parents and vocational challenges of midlife.

> **Ryan:** I lost my parents early, at ages twenty-seven and thirty-six. Grief is tough to get through. You have to choose joy in the grief, but you also have to move through grief in order to feel joy. In my experience, the ability to grieve and feel joy is the same muscle.

In addition to finding joy in the middle of dealing with the loss of my parents, I'm now fighting for joy as I process some work-related issues. Specifically, how can I find joy and not feel trapped by my professional decisions? There's a lot of existential pain to work through. Because my parents died so early, I wonder, *Am I on the downslope already? Is this it?*

At midlife, I understand that I've made some bad choices and, as a result, know that some things I wanted to happen might not. It's hard to find joy in the midst of that. It's easier to be joyful if you feel optimistic, but optimism is the gift of youth.

So many men at this age have been holding it together for so long, just keeping the hamster wheel spinning, that the psychic wear and tear is simply too much. We die a little every day in that space. I'm making the active choice to appreciate this life and all that is good in it rather than focus on what I don't have or won't achieve.

I've watched people who could easily fix things in their marriage but instead decide to throw it all away and start again. There's something about being a man under pressure that makes you think success is very binary.

It somehow seems safer to fail at everything and just reboot, such as with bankruptcy. You just move on and get to be happy. This is an American myth and it's very costly, especially when applied to marriage.

Ryan and Natasha continue to make proactive choices, such as bringing creativity into their relationship to avoid the pitfalls common in middle age.

> **Ryan:** We see our marriage as an art project. We work on our marriage prescriptively so that we're not just fixing things. Every year, we go on a marriage retreat. Sometimes it's really deep, and other times we don't connect with the content, so we just spend more time in bed.
>
> Whether it's children, food, parties, vacation, or a fund-raiser to end sex trafficking, collaborating is central to our marriage. That emphasis to build from within is really different than trying to fix something.
>
> **Natasha:** We also creatively love people. I see a need, and Ryan marshals the resources. We can be extravagant in our desire to show others God's love. What we do together is so much more amazing than what I could do by myself.

Ryan: Ultimately, the joy in our marriage is about healing—healing such things as being alone, being abandoned, not being worthy. The joy helps us comfort each other at a deep level.

Ryan and Natasha's lives overflow with that purposeful joy. They are an inspiration to Christopher and me as well as to the many others in their life.

During our twenty-five years together, joy has lifted us up and over many obstacles. It has given us a kingdom perspective and helped us not take ourselves so seriously. When I think back to our son and daughter-in-law's wedding, I have no doubt that our experience would have been completely different had we not chosen joy. "Joy is a far more dynamic, forceful weapon than most of us realize. The abiding sense that you are fiercely loved by God? *That* kind of joy empowers you to rise above any circumstance."[9] We all need that assurance as we face the inevitable challenges of life. Thankfully, our heavenly Father is well aware of this reality and generously provides His joy to strengthen and sustain us on the journey.

Going Deeper

1. How do you and your spouse actively choose joy, both individually and as a couple? What are some of your current barriers to it?

2. What's your take on James 1:2–4? Bring to mind a challenge or difficulty that's present in your marriage. What blocks you from finding joy in the midst of this?

3. Of the three ways to fight for joy—worship, prayer, and expressing gratitude—which is the easiest for you? Which is the most difficult? If you don't already, how might you and your spouse incorporate worship and prayer into your marriage?

4. If this is not already a practice in your marriage, become intentional about expressing your gratitude to God and to your spouse. It could be as simple as, "Thanks for filling up my gas tank" or "I so appreciate that you called to see if I needed anything from the store." Trust me. These add up.

5. If you struggle to believe in God's faithfulness and goodness, consider praying the following Scriptures on a regular basis: Psalm 139; Isaiah 54:1–10; 62:3–5; Lamentations 3; John 16:16–24; Romans 8:28; and 1 John 3:1. Allow the sacred words to guide your prayers. As you pray, ask God to increase your faith.

10

IT'S NOT GOOD
TO BE ALONE

The Complex Gift of Community

Without the love and support of multiple communities, Christopher and I would never have reconnected. When he unexpectedly broke off our first engagement, compassionate men and women helped us heal. One brave friend came over and sang worship songs with her arms wrapped around me. Her laments unleashed a torrent of tears. Christopher's closest comrades hung out with him for meals and impromptu jam sessions, giving him the opportunity to talk about what happened without trying to fix him.

These saints provided comfort, but because they understood what constitutes true healing, they also implored us to forgive when they detected bitterness and encouraged us to move forward when they detected we were stuck in regret. Their accountable love continually pointed us back to God, which allowed us to reconnect years down the road. Thanks to community, reconciliation was possible.

Our wedding was a massive community undertaking. Friends and family members baked our cake, made my dress, photographed the ceremony, led worship, organized and brought food, and even offered us a beach condo for our honeymoon. Thanks to community, our wedding was abundant, beautiful—and inexpensive.

Our reliance upon friends and family during our breakup and in the process of getting married foreshadowed what we have since learned to be true: if we want to become more like Jesus, and if we want our marriages to reflect His love, we must stitch ourselves into healthy communities. For though we each vow to love, honor, and cherish one person, being sewn into a relational patchwork of many people increases the likelihood that we will be able to uphold our vows.

Functional communities not only help us identify those areas where we need redemption but also offer us safe, nurturing environments in which to change. They curb any idolatrous tendencies, foster growth, and ease aloneness. Healthy communities also remind us that we cannot consistently love, serve, and sacrifice without ongoing help, both divine and human. (If we are reminded that we need God and others, we will be more likely to avail ourselves of them rather than muddle through under the myth of self-sufficiency.)

Though we might not always appreciate the ongoing challenges that are part of every community, they are nothing less than God's mercy and provision for us. Whether we're newly married or celebrating our golden anniversary, we need the complex gift of community.

What Does a Healthy Community Look Like? Hint: Just Like Marriage, It's Imperfect

Though no two communities look exactly the same, they share notable commonalities. When I use the term *community* in this chapter, I will be referring to a group of individuals who join together to worship and serve in Jesus's name. Healthy communities are comprised of diverse men and women—married and single—some of whom are intimate friends and others mere acquaintances, who want to grow. Because they long for transparency and transformation, they regularly confess their sins (James 5:16). In response to confession, a healthy community forgives, comforts, and, if necessary, corrects (2 Cor. 2:6–8). Rather than silence or dismiss questions and doubts, community members listen and validate (Heb. 10:25). They do not shy away from difficult conversations, conflicting opinions, or the inherent tensions of diversity (Eph. 4:2). Healthy communities willingly sacrifice their time and resources, even when it's not convenient (Acts 4:32–37). Finally, healthy communities accept us as we are *but also* call us into the fullness of Christ (Phil. 2:1–18).

Some of you are currently part of such communities. Your eyes are open wide to others' limitations, but you choose to stay because you see the community "cultivating together the resurrection life of Christ, by deeply and selflessly loving [one another]."[1] Others of you believe that *healthy community* is an oxymoron. Perhaps you have been betrayed or wounded within the context of a church. Christopher and I have worshipped with brothers and sisters who have breathed life into us, and we've been part of communities where unacknowledged brokenness sucked all the oxygen out of the sanctuary. One thing worth noting: just as in marriage, discouragement, disillusionment, and hurt are to be expected and are not necessarily reasons to leave.

Twentieth-century theologian and martyr Dietrich Bonhoeffer offered his insight regarding the complexity and, oddly enough, the necessity of being disappointed by community:

> Innumerable times a whole Christian community has broken down because it had sprung from a wish dream. The serious Christian, set down for the first time in a Christian community, is likely to bring with him a very definite idea of what Christian life together should be and to try to realize it. But God's grace speedily shatters such dreams. Just as surely as God desires to lead us to a knowledge of genuine Christian fellowship, so surely must we be overwhelmed by a great disillusionment with others, with Christians in general, and, if we are fortunate, with ourselves....
>
> Christian [community] is not an ideal which we must realize; it is rather a reality created by God in Christ in which we may participate.[2]

When we enter into community, we have unspoken longings for others to accept, appreciate, and affirm us. Others unintentionally dash these expectations, often without even knowing it. The same dynamic that happens in marriage also happens in community: our flaws and weaknesses get exposed, prompting us to either attack or retreat (while often making unfavorable conclusions about the one who wounded us). I not only withdraw but sulk for good measure. I can be an exemplary follower of Christ on the days when I'm alone in my office writing about being an exemplary follower of Christ. It's when I'm with people that my immaturity becomes evident.

Whenever these scenarios unfold, they provide us with a holy opportunity. Will we allow the circumstances to humble us and teach us how to bear with one another in love—or not? Occasionally, a community becomes so toxic that we need to walk away, but staying and allowing our roots to descend often yields more fruit than transplanting the tree.

Do We Really Need Community? Yes, and Here's Why

The marriage script in *The Book of Common Prayer* invites wedding guests to answer a simple but consequential question: "Will all of you witnessing these promises do all in your power to uphold these two persons in their marriage?"[3] Hopefully, the guests heartily proclaim, "We will!" During our wedding, the response to this question rocked the sanctuary, so much so that the pastor asked everyone to say it again. Perhaps based on our earlier challenges, they intuited that we might need to lean on their enthusiastic support in the years to come. Christopher and I are not alone in that need. All of us benefit from three unique ways that communities serve marriage: they reorient us away from idolatrous tendencies, they encourage us in our spiritual growth, and they offer us much-needed companionship.

1. Healthy Communities Keep Our Idolatrous Tendencies in Check

God created us to worship. If we don't worship the Creator, we worship the created, making idols in the process (see Rom. 1). I don't know anyone who has literally crafted or bowed down to golden statues as the Israelites did (see Exod. 32), but idolatrous practices emerge today as we attempt to meet our needs apart from God.

In round one of our relationship, I played the part of the idolater by refusing to acknowledge Christopher's weaknesses and limitations. I preferred to view him as the perfect husband-to-be who would satisfy all my relational and sexual needs. In return, he played the role of the idol, willingly receiving my adoration. Author and speaker Andrew Comiskey describes our idolatrous tendencies:

> Out of the broken, unaffirmed heart flow distorted desires and misbegotten schemes to secure love.... Not knowing who we are or how to secure love, we create idols. We bypass the Creator and bow down before images that appear to offer us completion.[4]

Mind you, I had no idea I was guilty of breaking the first and second commandments. It took two years of counseling for me to understand that I was expecting things from Christopher that only God could provide.

My habit of bending toward false gods is not unique. We live in an idolatrous age with larger-than-life personalities—inside and outside the church—who beckon us to bow down at their altars. After we lift them onto their pedestals, we protect their elevated position by offering them our loyalty. More often than not, we fail to understand that it's our fear, insecurity, and pride that motivate our behavior. We gain purpose and status by polishing our idols' pedestals, and the idols pay us back by acknowledging our presence from time to time. This warped dynamic always ends with the idol crashing down and shocked idolaters scurrying to safety.

As our early relationship illustrates, idolaters gravitate toward narcissists:

> Maybe I (Christopher) should interject here. Dorothy's casting of herself as a relational idolater might imply that my role of choice is the narcissist. I want to confirm that I agree.
>
> Truth be told, I care more about my own comfort than anybody else's, including my wife and sons, and it is for this reason that I'm not done needing a Savior or a church community. The refusal of other people to bow down and submit to my every whim is a divine mercy. I praise God for my detractors, especially those in the church, because they help me to be a better husband, father, and worship leader.

As we become part of a functional community, those of us who tend toward narcissism get pulled back to terra firma when others disagree with us or refuse to bow down. Those of us who tend toward idolizing the narcissist are called to look beyond the object of our adulation to the God who saves. A diverse weekly gathering that includes corporate confession, worship, and communion draws all of us to the holy center and calls us all into a larger story that revolves around Jesus, not us.

2. Healthy Communities Encourage Us to Grow

Healthy communities create a palpable accountability that inspires growth. Take the following scenario. Christopher and I have an argument on Saturday night, and due to some combination of fatigue and stubbornness, we fail to reconcile before church starts the next morning. As he directs the congregation to either reconcile any ongoing conflicts or abstain from communion (see Matt. 5:23–24), we both know we have a choice to make. Do we ignore Scripture and take communion, pretending that all is well? Or do we make eye contact across the sanctuary, silently agree that we'll be having a long conversation that afternoon, and abstain? Such moments of public mortification kill off the false self and lead to a life of integrity.

There's a drill my college field-hockey team did that illustrates the power of community to help us mature. We had to sprint from one goal line to the opposite end line and back in less than fifty seconds. If the last player did not cross the line before the coach's timer went off, we had to repeat the drill. One teammate was slow and often caused us to finish over time. Rather than resent her, we devised a strategy. Though she always placed herself at the end of the line, we moved her to the middle *and then all held hands.* We were a team, and we won or lost as a team. A church community that functions with this level of camaraderie and commitment will serve as a catalyst for transformation.

3. Healthy Communities Offer Us Companionship

Being part of a community eases our aloneness. When we marry, we seldom realize that we will sporadically feel a peculiar kind of loneliness. In the midst of our year-ten rough patch, I remember lying in bed less than a foot away from Christopher and feeling as though we might as well have been on opposite sides of the Continental Divide.

In the process of working through that difficult season, we decided to start a couples' group at our church. The weekly meeting included worship, teaching, and same-gendered small groups. Regardless of the topic, at the end of the night, someone always said, "I thought we were the only ones struggling with this." Listening to one another's stories thwarts the Enemy's scheme to isolate and shame us into silence. It also reduces the stigma of asking for help.

Inviting others in and finding support are crucial components of a thriving marriage, especially if you and your spouse are not on the same page spiritually or if one of you is less interested in transformation. I have multiple friends who find themselves in this situation.

Lisa and Patrick have been married for more than thirty-five years. Neither of them was a believer when they married, but not long after, Lisa made a commitment to follow Jesus. She is a radical, lay-down-my-life-for-the-kingdom kind of Christian. This contributes to the marriage's complexity. Lisa longs for spiritual companionship with Patrick, but her husband is unable to provide for these needs.

In a recent conversation, Lisa explains how she fills that gap:

> I deeply rely upon a community of believing friends to pray for and stand with me, particularly when I am struggling. They are a sounding board and a safe place where I can share honestly without the fear of rejection or reprisal. I don't have that freedom in my marriage.

Mei and David have been married for more than two decades. They are both believers, but they don't share the same perspective about how their faith is meant to shape their daily lives. This has been a source of pain and confusion for Mei, who assumed they would grow side by side. For some couples, this results in non-stop friction, disgruntlement, or even divorce. Mei is determined to avoid these snares and instead chooses to be grateful and love David as unselfishly as she is able. This resolve has deepened her faith. According to Mei,

> There are so many good things in our marriage. David is a super loving, incredibly generous

man who is very present to our children. We
are finding grace even though we still disagree
about what Christianity asks of us. Our edges
are gradually softening and diminishing. I'm
also learning that I'm not in control of the marriage. In fact, I have to ask myself, *What am I
in control of?* Our early marital crisis took us on
a path that I never imagined traveling. It was
awful, but I finally began to see that it was me
and Jesus, not just me. I'm now leaning on Him
rather than on David. And in the process, I'm
also working on my heart issues and trying to be
less judgmental and more vulnerable.

For Lisa and Mei, choosing to honor their marital vows despite
their disappointments has been challenging. Their friends' willingness to support them has alleviated their aloneness and enabled
them to love their husbands well.

Create the Community You Need

Initiate

In a fully redeemed world, every community would have a finely
tuned radar for distress and dispatch someone to arrive at our front
door, gluten-free casserole in hand, offering to pray before we've
even tweeted about our need. I don't know about you, but that's
not been our experience.

When Christopher and I were in the midst of our meltdown, we vulnerably laid out our challenges and frustrations to another couple who were also leaders in the church. Despite our obvious rawness and direct request for help, they never checked in with us. As in never. Perhaps that was because we were perceived to be the resident marriage experts and our struggle intimidated them. Maybe they were simply too busy. The easiest thing would have been for Christopher and me to fake it until the storm blew over.

Instead, we not only started the couples' group but also asked the pastor who officiated our wedding and his wife to pray with us. (And to be clear, we met with them repeatedly.)

Sometimes community happens organically. We stumble into a church or a neighborhood and find ourselves immersed in a relationally rich network. Other seasons bring relational famine and we go to bed hungry. More often than not, we need to seek out trustworthy, like-minded people and invite them deeper into relationship. Not all of you will have the time and resources to initiate a church-wide small group as we did. However, you don't have to be an officially sanctioned leader to invite friends over for dessert. (As a side note, it's healthy and helpful to include mature singles in such gatherings.) By sitting around a table and sharing food, conversation will flow and friendship will follow. Once there's enough familiarity and trust, test the waters to see how others will handle an honest disclosure or a plea for help.

Jonathan, whom you met in chapter 8, has now been meeting with the same three men once a month for fifteen years. They started face-to-face, and when he went to Africa, they continued over Skype. They intentionally ask personal questions and end by praying for each other. I've been getting together with my three bridesmaids once a quarter for twenty-four years. Over a meal, we catch up, keep each other accountable, and try to love each other well.

Christopher and I have learned not to expect anyone else to intuit our needs. We take responsibility to ask for whatever support, counsel, and practical help we lack. This takes courage and humility. We have to be willing to deal a deathblow to our pride. Pretending not to be needy is so much safer and more socially acceptable. There's risk involved with expressing need. After we bare our souls, will others label us as needy and avoid us at the next social gathering? Will they offer brilliant theological insights such as "God always works things together for your good"? It's highly probable that the aforementioned will happen. But if we ask for help anyway, we learn to articulate our needs rather than resent others for not meeting them. We also mature immeasurably in the process.

Shape

Shaping a community is slightly more challenging than initiating. Groups and organizations do not magically become dynamic and healthy. We need to leaven our communities with the necessary ingredients to make them safe, honest, and grace filled. This takes intentionality and patience.

Once, in the midst of a gathering of church leaders, the moderator asked a personal question about how we were doing. Without hesitating, I answered honestly. Someone took advantage of that vulnerability and made a joke. Half the room laughed. The half that didn't laugh intuited an important lesson—namely, this is not a safe place to be emotionally vulnerable. That metamessage could have been prevented if the leader had created ground rules or in the moment had said something along the lines of "Laughter is great but not at another's expense. Let's avoid that kind of comment from here on."

Something Christopher and I have noticed after thirty years of leading: people tend to grow more when the community values honesty and vulnerability. Far too often, when others ask how we're doing, we respond with one vague word: *fine*. I'm fine. Marriage is fine. Parenting is fine. Our intimate and spiritual lives are fine. Sometimes it's socially appropriate to be vague. Sometimes, like my experience in that small group, we need to protect ourselves. In other situations, we might be dodging our painful realities because we're scared others will reject us if they know what a mess we are.

Years ago Christopher and I were having dinner with friends when the wife made a somewhat disparaging comment about their sex life. I tuned in and asked, "Are things going okay in the bedroom?" They looked at each other and then he said, "Not so much." When I asked if they wanted to say more, they admitted they had not been intimate for more than six years. They divorced not long after. I'm not advocating that we casually inquire about our friends' sex lives over a cappuccino at the local café, though I will say that when we talk about sex, the normal pretense disappears. By asking a direct question such as "How's your marriage?" and admitting when ours isn't doing so well, we create an opening for dialogue. We also increase the likelihood that honesty and vulnerability will become normative.

Perhaps the only sane way we can uphold those values is if we have some confidence that others will continue to love us as we reveal our weaknesses and struggles. If we experience reprisal, betrayal, or judgment, we will quickly learn to hide our failures and pretend that we're fine. Healthy communities must exhibit grace and faithfully forgive because none of us are perfect.

Model and Validate Need

When the Holy Spirit convicted Christopher that he needed to confess his sexual addiction, it took him three years to push past his fear of being rejected and go for it. When he finally risked telling his story to two other men, he learned something unexpected: forgiveness and grace have the power to break shame. The response of his friends allowed him to experience unconditional love and subsequently bolstered him to fight for more freedom. Over time, he discovered that his transparency invited other men to be equally honest.

Healthy communities encourage us to ask for help. They expect that hard questions will be asked and train their leaders not to respond with Christian platitudes. Conversely, unhealthy communities value pretense, dismiss weakness, discourage confession of sins, and will not advocate getting professional help.

Because they do not dismiss or judge neediness, healthy communities care for those who are weak or powerless. They will never, under any circumstances, make excuses for or justify emotional, verbal, or physical abuse or any form of coercion. Any community—religious or secular—that blames victims for their mistreatment typically cares more about protecting those in power than protecting those who are vulnerable. If you find yourself in this situation, seek immediate help from those outside the institution.

Paul and Barbara's Story

Remember the pastor who tried to soften the results of our personality test? That was Paul. The couple who helped us during our year-ten crisis? Paul and his wife, Barbara. They are humble servants, no-nonsense truth tellers, and committed members of several different communities. I asked them to flesh out the role of community in supporting and sustaining marriage.

> **Paul:** When we first got married, we were part of a weekly Bible study with six other couples. It was there that we got to know the couple who would become our best friends. Ten years later, we decided to build a duplex together in a largely abandoned area of Boston.
>
> This decision was significant. We'd get our kids to bed and the other husband and I would play Nerf basketball or table tennis. I could take the baby monitor over when I went to pick up

Barbara from work. Sharing the two-family house was like having a large family. It was the single most important thing that stabilized us during our early years.

As Paul and Barbara's family increased in size—they have eight children—they outgrew the duplex but decided to build another home around the corner from their friends. Not long after this move, Barb's mom, who had been diagnosed with multiple sclerosis, came to live with them.

Barbara: Because we already had six kids at the time, we did not initially think we'd have mom with us, but then it became clear that it was either the nursing home or our home. We had health aides come on a rotating basis, but it was really my sisters and my neighbors who came twice a week to feed her and put her to bed who made this possible. Because the kids were also involved in her care, we had this shared experience of being faithful to the Lord in stewarding my mom's life. It was extraordinary.

That said, receiving from others has been hard. I know it's countercultural to have eight children, and I can easily feel that I'm a bit of a burden. Part of the reason we said yes to having a large family, yes to caring for my mom, and yes to pastoring in the city was it helped us become aware of our needs. Had we played it safe, we would not have been aware of our neediness and would not have turned to those around us.

Quite honestly, I'd rather do everything myself, but that leaves me feeling pretty isolated. My deep desire to connect drives me to these places of vulnerability. If you are going to be my friend, it's got to be okay that I'm going to lean on you.

Paul's and Barbara's connections to community are multi-faceted. Not only have they lived in the same neighborhood for twenty-nine years, but Paul has coached athletic teams for many seasons and Barbara has been part of a homeschooling co-op. These extensive connections have provided them with many opportunities to serve and be served. They have also provided opportunities to work through conflicts.

Paul: We've had numerous conflicts in our community—conflicts that we've worked through, conflicts that have resulted in separation and that were reconciled over time, but also conflicts that were never healed. Early on in our relationship with our housemates, we had a few ugly fights. We believed that it was important to talk about what was going on rather than deny any issues.

Barbara: We made it through the challenges. We've come through stronger, and it expanded our capacity to love. All of these conflicts have made us slow to judge and quick to be generous. We've seen what bitterness does, and we don't want that. The remedy is repentance and forgiveness.

Paul: Real community is hard work, and one can't always get it right. But it's been an essential component to our marriage's success.

Barbara: I can't meet every one of Paul's needs, nor can he meet all of mine. I learned how to golf and we hike together, but he wants to play basketball and football. If he does that with friends, then it frees me to do the things with him that I enjoy. Rather than feeling like I'm disappointing him, I think this is healthy. Conversely, though Paul is faithful in praying with me, he cannot meet the quantity of my need for prayer. That's where my friends come in. We give each other freedom to seek out others in the community to meet needs that are not specific to marriage.

Paul and I enjoy a remarkably loving and happy marriage. I think a major reason for this is the blessing of having a community to support and encourage us through the years. When we reflect upon our life together, we agree that by God's grace we are living out our favorite movie, *It's a Wonderful Life*. The support and love I've felt from so many friends has made those seemingly impossible seasons not only bearable but also amazing. I just can't imagine what life would be like without community.

Supportive communities helped bring Christopher and me back together and have helped us stay together. This is as it should be. When marriages and communities are functioning properly, they create a dynamic synergy. Marriages benefit from the structure, diversity, and accountability that communities offer, and communities benefit from the vulnerability, commitment, and stability that characterize marriage. Healthy marriages become one of the cornerstones of healthy communities. The many individuals who comprise a healthy community act like mortar, filling in the gaps and preventing the harsh elements and the devious Enemy from penetrating our union.

In Jonathan Wilson-Hartgrove's book *The Wisdom of Stability*, he affirms, "Life with the God we know in Jesus Christ is lived in community with other people. We can only grow into the fullness of what we are made to be in Christ by opening ourselves to the particular brothers and sisters who mediate Christ's presence to us."[5] We move incrementally toward that fullness when we "trust Jesus enough to stay"[6]—in our marriages and also in our communities. It's in the failing, forgiving, serving, and sacrificing that we learn what it means to faithfully love and, by God's grace, actually do it.

Going Deeper

1. When you're struggling, do you ask for help? If not, what holds you back? Are you willing to ask for help from people who might challenge you, or do you tend to seek out those who are more sympathetic?

2. How honest are you with your closest friends? Could you to take it up a notch?

3. Are you part of a healthy community? If so, what's your unique contribution to that community? If you are not currently part of a community, explore what that is costing you.

4. How does your community support marriage? If it doesn't, how could you move your community in that direction?

MADE BEAUTIFUL

The Redemptive Power of Sacrificial Love

Regardless of what triggered Christopher's occasional shame attacks, the only thing that seemed remotely helpful was for me to give him a wide berth. In the middle of one particularly intense attack, I managed to extend grace for three days, a personal record, but then my patience wore thin. I wanted him to snap out of it. Maybe I even said as much. Not surprisingly, my so-called encouragement failed to help.

That night as I was getting ready for bed, I vented to the Lord. I immediately sensed the Holy Spirit respond, "Invite Christopher to make love tonight." My less-than-sanctified reply was, "No! Please! Not that!" Let me explain. Christopher is an amazing lover. He's patient, generous, and every bit as committed to my pleasure as his own. It wasn't that our intimate life was in any way unpleasant. At the beginning of our marriage, we had made a commitment to be emotionally present in the bedroom. Because I felt so annoyed with him, I did not want to be emotionally—or physically—present; I wanted to check out and read a book.

I admitted as much to God but then asked Him to make me willing. And He did. When Christopher climbed into bed, I inquired if he wanted to be intimate, half hoping he would say no. He was taken aback but said yes. It was a memorable night. My willingness to follow God's lead and do what I did not want to do had a powerful impact. In Christopher's words:

> Prior to this breakthrough, my shame attacks sometimes lasted for days. During these bouts, I would be convinced that my physical limitations and character flaws were the dominant reality of my being. These deep pockets of distorted thinking, which were reinforced by two incidents of molestation as a teen, labeled me as irrevocably flawed and unworthy of affection. So when Dorothy expressed her desire to be sexually intimate with me, I was humbled and shocked. I knew I was being deliberately unpleasant. I could not have predicted the flood of tears that surfaced during our time together.
>
> Dorothy's gift of love in the face of my unloveliness brought about a radical and permanent change in my ability to resist these shame attacks. Now I can tell when they are about to occur, I'm aware of what precipitated them, and I'm able to navigate out of them within a few hours. I attribute this to Dorothy's choice to obey God and sacrificially love me.

I don't include this story to congratulate myself. God deserves all the credit. Despite the reality that I obviously wanted Christopher to stop being so toxic, I wasn't interceding for him. In fact, I hoped he would cheer up on his own. But God knew that he needed horizontal as well as vertical intervention. Because I had enough faith to believe that our Father would empower me to love, I ventured in. As a result, the kingdom broke into our marriage and changed us. Christopher and I look back on that night as evidence that we don't need to be perfect to love sacrificially; we simply need to be willing.

I wrote in chapter 1, "What differentiates a loving, joyful, intimate marriage from a disappointing, frustrating one is the willingness and commitment to be changed, to say yes to God's transforming work, and to become increasingly holy with each passing year." I hope I've made it clear that transformation is a lifelong process that's equal parts hard work, faithful waiting, and supernatural intervention. Though miracles do abound, we never become saints—in the truest sense of the word—overnight.

If our experience is at all typical, transformation happens at a glacial pace. Becoming holy is slow and arduous because we're stubborn sinners but also because being transformed into the image of Christ is meant to change every aspect of our lives.

Gary Thomas writes in *Sacred Marriage*, "Holiness is far more than an *inclination* toward occasional acts of kindness and charity. It is a commitment to persistent surrender before God."[1] Each time we wave the white flag signifying the surrender of self, God assumes command of our rebel outpost and immediately hoists a banner signaling the advent of His kingdom. As the years go by and the King's territory expands, He enables us to love our spouses joyfully and sacrificially.

The Nature of Sacrificial Love

God's love is not theoretical; it's a crown of thorns pressed into Jesus's brow, nails driven through sinew and bones, and ultimately, His brutal death. First John 3:16 reads, "We know what real love is because Jesus gave up his life for us." Few of us will literally die for our spouses. Instead, we will be asked to lay down our agendas, our preferences, and sometimes even our dreams. Marlena Graves gently reminds us, "Our love too has to be a tangible love, not a theoretical love."[2]

God offers us opportunities to tangibly and sacrificially love our spouses on a daily, if not hourly, basis. We love when we apologize for our harshness rather than pretend it didn't happen. We love when we push past our fatigue and serve each other at the end of an exhausting week. We love as we extend grace, perhaps particularly when they have done nothing to deserve it.

In every marriage, there are obvious sacrifices that anyone who's paying attention will notice. Paul, whom you met in the previous chapter, has become a property manager in addition to being a full-time pastor so that he can provide additional income for their family. This occasionally drains him physically and emotionally.

There are also hidden sacrifices that no one else ever witnesses. Both forms of sacrifice are costly, but the hidden sacrifices seem even more so. This is in part because we receive no recognition for our efforts. Due to my ongoing health issues, Christopher repeatedly forfeits his needs on my behalf. He understands that if it's past nine thirty at night, it's unlikely that I will be able to engage in any kind of meaningful conversation—or be interested in having sex. I know that my limitations disappoint him, but he has never made me feel guilty. That's sacrificial love.

Every couple included in this book loves in these unseen ways. Only Samantha and Evan understand how he voluntarily gives up the safe haven of a single-culture home to embrace her culture and how she has learned to esteem his Chinese heritage. Such acts of love are fragrant offerings, much like when Mary poured nard on Jesus's feet (Luke 7:36–38).

Jesus Christ is the ultimate reference point for what it means to love sacrificially. His obedience cost Him everything: His reputation, His well-being, His comfort, His life, and—when He gave up His spirit—even His connection to God the Father (Matt. 27:46). Sacrificial love is never cheap, nor does it happen coincidentally. It's a countercultural choice that we have to willingly and repeatedly make.

How Is Such Love Possible?

Connect to the Source

How do we offer this countercultural love to our spouses? First, we experience God's love for ourselves and then learn to depend on His faithful provision.

If we have not personally experienced God's love, trying to give it away is like trying to describe the taste of a perfectly ripe peach when we have never bitten into the fruit's juicy flesh. Though we seldom dwell on this reality, we love because God first loved us (1 John 4:19). He created us with a primal longing to receive His love. This longing takes up residence in our souls and compels us to seek after the source. Author Andrea Dilley shares what compelled her to search after God in *Faith and Other Flat Tires*:

> To me, longing for God was like hearing music from an open window on the street or seeing mountains off in the distance. The yearning felt almost like grief. A cry born into my heart before the human heart ever existed. A desire so deep and far back that it seemed almost prehistoric. I sensed the *imago Dei*, the image of God within me.... I was a homing bird traveling with my outspread wings, carried by an innate compass and crossing a thousand miles to get back to the place where I began.[3]

This gnawing, ever-present need for love is what made many of us turn to God in the first place. The imperfect, inconsistent love we receive from our parents and our siblings, from our friends and our spouses, only whets our appetites to the possibility of something more satisfying. Through painful trial and error, we learn that the perfect version can be found only in Christ. As we regularly receive His love, it empowers and emboldens us to offer it to others.

To remain on the path of transformation and continue to love our spouses sacrificially, we must stay connected to God. His love is not meant to be a onetime download. We need regular, even daily, upgrades. Jesus's instruction to His disciples applies to us today:

> Remain in me, and I will remain in you. For a branch cannot produce fruit if it is severed from the vine, and you cannot be fruitful unless you remain in me.
>
> Yes, I am the vine; you are the branches. Those who remain in me, and I in them, will produce much fruit. For apart from me you can do nothing. (John 15:4–5)

Several years back, a freakishly early snowstorm hit New England. Because we had not experienced a killing frost, most of the trees still had their leaves. The heavy, wet snow gathered on those leaves all night, and throughout the morning, we could hear limbs snap off and land with a thud. It was a devastating storm. In the weeks that followed, the life-fluid gradually drained out of the downed limbs, and the leaves became brown and shriveled. We too will wither and become brittle if we disconnect from God. Connection happens through the more obvious spiritual disciplines, such as worship, prayer, and reading Scripture, but also through serving others and drinking in the beauty of His creation.

By staying connected to the Father, we not only receive His love but also discern how He is at work in our beloved's life. He gives us the capacity to see beyond our spouses' present limitations and preexisting wounds so that we can affirm God's call even when the clouds of doubt obscure their vision. After speaking words of hope over our spouses, we then walk shoulder to shoulder, in sickness and in health, in poverty and in abundance, to help them realize that call.

Remember Jon and Amy from chapter 3 who approached marriage as a partnership? Jon not only encouraged Amy to attend grad school but then supported her emotionally and practically. More than a decade ago, Christopher made what seemed like a ridiculous suggestion to me: "I wonder if you should think about writing." I believe that God gave him that seed, which he planted and faithfully watered. Adopting this missional mind-set for our spouses and our marriages allows us to let go of the faulty assumption that our primary objective is making each other happy. There's much more at stake and that more will keep us engaged and connected until we draw our final breath.

Eradicate Any and All Hierarchies

During his life on earth, Jesus dismantled worldly hierarchies by asking those in positions of power to step down and make space for the oppressed. We need to follow His example in our marriages and eradicate any inequitable power dynamics so that both spouses have equal access to Jesus. This means that some of us will need to abdicate our self-made thrones (e.g., controlling the terms of the marriage) and others will need help breaking free from thought and behavioral patterns that create barriers between us and God (e.g., believing the false narrative that we don't have the right to be a full partner).

At the core of what it means to be people of the cross is the concept of "one-downmanship."[4] Mike Mason describes this as

> a backwards tug of war between two wills each equally determined not to win. That is really the only attitude that works in marriage because that is the way the Lord designed it.... For "He must increase, but I must decrease," declared John the Baptist of Jesus (John 3:30), and that is the fate of all of us: We must all diminish for the glory of God.[5]

The apostle Paul articulates this in his letter to the Philippians:

> Don't be selfish; don't try to impress others. Be humble, thinking of others as better than yourselves. Don't look out only for your own interests, but take an interest in others, too.
>
> You must have the same attitude that Christ Jesus had. (Phil. 2:3–5)

In healthy marriages, one-downmanship can take many forms. Christopher accepted more clients so that he could compensate for my loss of income as I wrote this book. For the interracial couple Matt and Li (from chapter 4), one-downmanship has meant Li shouldering a greater portion of the parenting so that Matt could progress professionally. Though it makes no sense, as we find specific ways to diminish for the sake of loving

232 MAKING MARRIAGE BEAUTIFUL

our spouses well, our joy and contentment increase. Singer-songwriter Audrey Assad nailed it when she wrote, "We will never have true joy if we do not lay ourselves down for something or someone."[6]

The potential problem with this philosophy is that unless both husband and wife equally commit, someone might be taken advantage of or, in the worst-case scenario, abused. In every marriage, there will be seasons when one spouse sacrifices more than the other. This is to be expected. It should not become normative. Although the essential message of one-downmanship is true for all believers, it could be counterproductive for those who incessantly diminish themselves. This might be the case if you struggle with self-hatred, if your spouse is an addict not pursuing recovery, or if you have been taught that you need to submit to your spouse regardless of the cost to your well-being.

It's hugely important to differentiate between healthy, God-honoring one-downmanship and surrendering in an inequitable or domineering relationship. For those of you in the latter situation, one-downmanship does not mean that you should tuck in and ignore your needs. You will have to refute the Enemy's lies that you are less than. When you've been repeatedly lied to, it can be difficult to discern truth from fiction. At the risk of being overly simplistic, the Enemy tears down; Jesus builds up. The Enemy shames; Jesus lovingly rebukes. The Enemy tells us we are worthless; Jesus makes us worthy through His sacrificial death. If you are continuously demeaned, belittled, or threatened by your spouse, I urge you to seek professional help.

How Can We Sustain This Sacrificial Love for the Long Haul?

Being on the receiving end of sacrificial love is amazing. However, as many of you know, giving sacrificial love can expose our limitations like nothing else. In order to succeed for the long haul, we need grace, mercy, patience, humor, shared mission, and intimacy.

Grace

Grace is favor: something delightful that is completely undeserved, unexpected, and freely given. For example, salvation is a gift from God that we cannot earn (Eph. 2:5–9). Grace helps us grow in sacrificial love because it reminds us that our spouses do not owe us anything. Because we are recipients of God's generous grace, can we offer any less to our husbands or wives?

In the context of our marriages, we have regular opportunities to extend grace by going beyond what's expected to bless our spouses. Barbara extends grace to Paul when she encourages him to go play golf even though she would rather spend the morning praying together. Grace is saying, "I know it's your turn to give the kids a bath/cook dinner/walk the dog, but I'll do it." Grace is easy when we're well resourced and not so easy when we're tired or stressed.

Mercy

Mercy carries with it connotations of being spared, pardoned, or forgiven for something we did or perhaps didn't do. It is a manifestation of kindness and love, particularly when something else is deserved. Referencing Titus 3:5, poet Luci Shaw writes, "Now, as we yield ourselves to be washed in grace's laundry, the scandal of undeserved mercy acts on us as God's unlikely bleach."[7] Yes and amen! The Lord is merciful to us even though we regularly break His commands and His heart. Extending mercy fosters sacrificial love because it prevents us from judging one another and hardening our hearts. It was mercy that motivated Cassandra to forgive and choose to keep loving Steven after he confessed the full extent of his sexual addiction.

Patience

Patience is one of nine fruits of the Spirit listed by the apostle Paul in Galatians 5:22–23, all of which are essential for marriage. Patience sustains sacrificial love because it allows us to wait for God to move rather than demanding results on our timetable. Patience is imperative when our communication styles vary or we come from different ethnic backgrounds. Because transformation cannot be hurried along, patience also means committing to stay—in a difficult conversation and also in the difficult seasons of marriage.

Christopher displays immeasurable patience with me as I battle chronic fatigue and fibromyalgia, and I extend patience to him by letting him process verbally. Sofia gives Mateo the gift of patience by granting him time alone to process their disagreements rather than demanding that he work it through immediately, which is her preference.

Humor

Humor functions like Miracle-Gro for sacrificial love. It nourishes and strengthens our scrawny seedlings of love, allowing them to grow increasingly robust. Assuming that we don't use humor as an escape from the hard work of growing and maturing, laughing at our limitations and mishaps helps us not to take ourselves too seriously.

Natasha and Ryan's ability to laugh together is part of what helps them be involved in such intense and demanding ministries. Christopher and I continue to guffaw at the rodent-infested cabin rental and the baby powder as a crime deterrent. It's taken me a while, but I have gradually learned that finding humor in my profound limitations reduces their sting. The other morning, I could not help but laugh at myself when I woke up. I had earplugs in, an eye mask on, one pillow over my head, my pajamas on inside out so the seams wouldn't irritate me, and a boot on to ease my plantar fasciitis. It's a good thing it's still dark when Christopher wakes up. If humor feels inaccessible, ask God to help you move in that direction. Then make a bowl of popcorn and watch Jimmy Fallon, Trevor Noah, Carol Burnett, Gilda Radner, or Lucille Ball.

Shared Mission

Focusing a portion of our time and energy on others allows us to be part of the larger world, which inevitably puts our issues in perspective. Referring to his marriage, pastor Francis Chan writes, "Being in war together is what keeps us from being at war with each other.... [Our] unity has come as a result of the mission. It has been a byproduct of serving the Lord."[8] As we serve and love those outside our four walls, the Lord expands our capacity to serve and love those under the same roof.

Being missional has always been a priority for Christopher and me. Five years after we got married, we initiated a long-term healing group in the Boston area. For more than twenty years now, we've partnered with others in offering instruction and healing to men and women on a variety of topics, including marriage, parenting, sobriety, and racial reconciliation. Though not everyone will have the option of leading out as we have, finding ways to serve side by side, perhaps with Habitat for Humanity or in local homeless shelters, is essential to the enduring health of our marriages. Jonathan and Talisa's choice to leave the States and serve the underserved in South Africa has bound them together in sacrificial love. As they extend themselves to others, their love has deepened.

Intimacy

God hardwired us to need and respond to loving touch. Touch is the first sense to develop and the last one we lose in the aging process. In a hypersexualized culture, touch tends to be limited to sex, and sex tends to be reduced to technique and pleasure rather than a unique type of sacrificial love.

Physical intimacy is actually a form of ministry and healing, especially as we age. Unconditional, non-shaming affection demonstrates to us that we are lovable and desirable, even when the world overlooks us. We do not need to have intercourse in order to be physically intimate, but we do need skin-to-skin contact to prevent our marriages from becoming a business partnership. Regardless of how we express affection, it should result in physical pleasure, increased trust, and emotional intimacy.

That said, touch and sexual intimacy may be particularly difficult for those who struggle from the effects of abuse or trauma. If you are an abuse victim, the journey to finding enjoyment in the bedroom may take years of intentionality and persistence. Certain situations, sensations, and kinds of touch may trigger memories and fear. Because shame is a consequence of abuse, you might feel conflicted; you want to enjoy your spouse, but touch causes you to shut down or feel angry or dirty. Honest communication and time spent with skilled therapists or counselors (the average pastor will generally not have sufficient experience or credentials) will be crucial to your healing. Though you might be tempted to fake it and deny your internal battle, doing so may limit your transformation.

If your spouse has a history of being abused, God will use you to be an agent of healing. By (1) assuring your husband or wife of your unconditional love, (2) respecting his or her boundaries, (3) extending patience and tenderness (particularly in the bedroom), and (4) communicating that you're not going anywhere *regardless of how long the healing takes*, you can help your spouse write a new narrative. You might feel frustrated or even exasperated by the length of time it takes to see evidence of healing. These are valid feelings. Nevertheless, harshness or indifference can compound the trauma of abuse and delay the kind of intimacy and pleasure you long for. Please don't give up. Your desire for authentic sexual intimacy might be the only reason you will continue to move forward as a couple.

Due to the shame that Christopher carried as a result of his molestation and his sexual addiction, the two of us did not have an effortless segue into marital sexuality. Whether it's due to abuse, addiction, or misguided church teaching, internalized shame complicates the experience of pleasure. Christopher had to push aside any distorted images and choose to be present *with me* each time we were intimate. That meant I had to adjust my expectations for what marital sexuality would look like and wait patiently for him to be ready.

Because of our commitment to grow, we now have an enjoyable and dynamic intimate life. Neither of us takes this for granted, nor do we assume that every bride and groom has arrived at the same destination. With this in mind, I will not prescribe how often couples should be intimate. The notion that we need to have sex a certain number of times every week in order to be considered normal seems artificial. (We also believe that the national average is skewed by the inclusion of college students!)

Our sexual desires have an ebb and flow connected to the demands of our days as well as our stages of life. Having teenagers who are up late, caring for elderly parents, and our own aging process all affect our sexuality. (At this point in our life, the spirit is generally willing but the flesh is often tired.) It's also important to note that we must faithfully steward our longings during certain seasons, such as military deployment or extended illnesses. Despite what contemporary cultures tell us, abstinence and self-control are possible. (Christopher notes, "Men, you will not die if you don't have regular orgasms.")

Christopher and I endeavor to be honest with each other regarding our desire for sex. Neither one of us has ever lied about having a headache. If we are indeed too tired or simply out of sorts, we give a soft no: "I'd love to be intimate with you, but I can't pull it off tonight. How about Saturday?" We try to balance the reality of our limitations with Paul's admonitions: "The husband should fulfill his wife's sexual needs, and the wife should fulfill her husband's needs" (1 Cor. 7:3).

We have noticed that sometimes, in our oversexed culture, the church can err on the side of putting pressure on a wife to satisfy her husband's sexual desires, regardless of her own needs or limitations. Our time in bed together is meant to be mutually desired, mutually honoring, and mutually affirming. It's not a birthright. On the other side of this equation, if we are rarely interested in being intimate, this may indicate an area in which we need the Lord's healing touch. Please ask for help: don't let shame or past hurts sabotage your intimate life.

The Geology of Marriage

As the Laurentide Glacier extended its reach into what is now New England, anything that could not withstand its force was pushed in a southern trajectory. When the ice finally stopped moving forward and began to recede, it left behind whimsically placed boulders and mucky glacial till. That till includes deposits of thick clay, sand, and millions of rocks. Farmers continue to pull these rocks from their fields today, adding them to the picturesque but mostly inefficient walls that delineate property lines.

We happen to live on glacial till. I love everything about our property, except the soil. The combination of rocks, clay, and sand creates a hostile environment for anything other than weeds and gangly oak and pine trees. Over the decade that we've called this home, I've attempted to transform the land with flowering shrubs and perennials. Because the soil is so poor, it's a slow process and one that cannot be abandoned without notable consequences.

Not long after I began writing this book, my father fell and broke his leg. He came through surgery and gained enough mobility to return home, but he never fully recovered and passed away a few months later. The time and energy that would have been directed to caring for my garden last spring and summer were directed toward my dad. By September, because of the combination of our poor soil and my neglect, weeds towered over my Jerusalem artichokes, an evil virus destroyed most of the weigela, and the beetles consumed the echinacea. Though I've been aware that gardens, like marriage, cannot flourish without constant, tender care, I had a visual reminder of this reality every time I turned into our driveway.

While finishing this chapter, it occurred to me: we are all attempting to grow and nurture our marriages in the cultural equivalent of glacial till. Our world is increasingly inhospitable to committed, sacrificial relationships. Not only are we encouraged to pursue happiness and self-fulfillment over sacrifice, but when we faithfully love each other, no one celebrates by applauding our efforts or offering us a cash bonus.

Like the gardeners here in New England, our motivation to make and sustain beautiful marriages must come from within. We have to commit—and then refuse to quit. Regardless of whether or not we feel like it. Regardless of whether anyone is noticing what we're doing or cheering us on.

Despite the sometimes lonely and seemingly Sisyphean nature of transformation, our Father does not want us to despondently abandon the work or soldier on in grim drivenness. Because He longs for our transformation more than we do, God not only provides us with an example of what it means to love but also offers us resurrection power (Eph. 1:19–20), increasing the likelihood of our success.

In the context of marriage, success comes after we work the soil, plant, water, and prune—in faith—year after year. The gradual transformation of our inner landscapes allows us to embrace each other in our flawed states and offer an imperfect, yet oh-so-sweet, love. It's mysterious but true that the very process of loving sacrificially leads to transformation, not only in the lover but also in the one loved.

Despite my many gardening failures, I do have one routine success: daffodils. Every fall, I dig down into our pathetic soil and drop these portents of hope into the damp earth. When one of our sons first watched me plant bulbs, he furrowed his brow and asked incredulously, "Why are you doing that?" Indeed.

Unless you have witnessed the remarkable transformation from wizened and seemingly dead to marvelously alive, it does seem foolish. But despite our impoverished soil and harsh winters, each spring, slender green shoots poke through the melting snow and quickly explode into a stunning display of faith fulfilled. I'm well aware that the daffodils' emergence and subsequent blooms have more to do with their DNA than with my skills as a gardener. Likewise, my love for Christopher has more to do with God's character than my own.

After twenty-five years of learning how to let Jesus transform me so that I can love Christopher well, I'd like to offer some advice: Keep clearing the rocks. Keep amending the soil and pulling the weeds. Keep planting your bulbs. As the seasons pass, your faithful obedience will result in the gradual transformation of your soul and your marriage. All will be made beautiful in time.

Blessings on the journey.

Dorothy and Christopher

Going Deeper

1. Where do you see God at work in your marriage, your life, and your spouse's life? Make sure you celebrate this and express your gratitude to each other and God.

2. Can you call to mind several specific times when you chose sacrificial love in order to bless your spouse? If not, consider asking God to help you develop in this area. Ask your spouse if there are any specific ways he or she would like to be served.

3. What are the relational weeds or boulders that God might be asking you to extricate? Ask God to bring you healing and wholeness in these areas. Pray for each other. Confess and forgive where appropriate.

4. What are the bulbs that God might be asking you to plant? Do you need more grace, mercy, patience, humor, shared mission, or intimacy?

5. How can you encourage your spouse to grow into the fullness of who God created him or her to be without controlling or manipulating? Does your spouse have a God-inspired dream that has yet to be fulfilled? How could you make sacrifices in order for this to happen?

6. Consider rereading this book in a year or two and note the places where God has broken in and the areas where you are still waiting. Don't give up!

ACKNOWLEDGMENTS

This book would not have happened without the support of the Redbud Community.

Special thanks to my agent, Karen Newmair of Credo Communications; Alice Crider, Abby DeBenedittis, Amy Konyndyk, and the rest of the excellent crew at David C Cook; Connie Gabbert, who designed the beautiful cover; the eight couples who bravely shared their stories; and Dr. Gary Chapman for writing the foreword.

I am indebted to the excellent editorial assistance of Jodi Steiner, for the earlier drafts, and Lisa Washington Lamb, for the later drafts. You both took my work to the next level.

To my Patreon and prayer team: the Tjernagels, Gretchen Saalbach, Val Cox, the Andrews, the Bjorcks, the MacDonalds, the Hodgkins, Robin Lake, Rachel Wilson, the Szatkowskis, the Choos, the Rays, Karen Stevenson, Barbara Brescia, Jessica Finch, Rebecca Bell, Chelsea Vessenes, the Frawleys, the Knights, Margaret Spellman Merrell, the Hildenbrands, Lisa Calderon, Erin Brehm, the Rowes, Cheryl Poole, Bernice Sim, Ben Knight, Sonia Andreson, Ann Armstrong, the Dennisons, the Wenzels, the Browns, Alexis Kruza, Annika Greco, Charlotte Gillespie, the

Taos, and Jean Henricksen. Special thanks to my neighbor Sue Roper, who has so often anticipated my needs and selflessly offered her time.

On the editorial side, there's always the risk of forgetting someone who helped me. If you don't see your name here, please know I am deeply grateful for your contributions and I'm so sorry I omitted your name. My early readers, copyeditors, and on-call editorial crew: Mary Yerkes, Katie James, Dr. Jeff Bjorck, Suzanne Burden, Annalaura M. Chaung, Andrew Comiskey, Catherine Carlson McNiel, Mardi Fuller, Tony Green, Paul Griffiths, Nancy Hodgkins, Sharon Hoover, Ray Kollbocker, Terri Kraus, Lara Krupicka, Bronwyn Lea, Leslie Leyland Fields, Aleah Marsden, Meadow Rue Merrill, Jen P. Michel, Sheila and Nick Rowe, Gretchen Saalbach, Amy Simpson, Margot Starbuck, Wendy Stringer, Dorcas Cheng-Tozun, Michelle Van Loon, and Jo Young.

To my friends who generously wrote endorsements, I am so very grateful.

On the home front, my parents, Phil Littell (who passed away as I was writing this), Virginia Cannon and her husband, Charles, for the years of support and encouragement; Matthew, for allowing me to miss so many of your athletic events and for your willingness to eat pizza at least twice a week; Anthony, Kate, and GianCarlo for consistently praying for me; and of course, to Christopher. My world would be diminished without your love, patience, and support.

NOTES

INTRODUCTION

1. Gary Thomas, *The Glorious Pursuit: Embracing the Virtues of Christ* (Colorado Springs, CO: NavPress, 1998), 42.

2. Ruth Haley Barton, *Life Together in Christ: Experiencing Transformation in Community* (Downers Grove, IL: InterVarsity Press, 2014), 11.

3. Mike Mason, *The Mystery of Marriage: Meditations on the Miracle* (Sisters, OR: Multnomah, 2005), 53.

4. Jen Pollock Michel, *Teach Us to Want: Longing, Ambition and the Life of Faith* (Downers Grove, IL: InterVarsity Press, 2014), 36.

CHAPTER 1: MARRIAGE WILL CHANGE YOU

1. Jen Pollock Michel, *Teach Us to Want: Longing, Ambition and the Life of Faith* (Downers Grove, IL: InterVarsity Press, 2014), 42.

2. Carolyn Custis James, *Malestrom: Manhood Swept into the Currents of a Changing World* (Grand Rapids, MI: Zondervan, 2015), 176.

3. Andrew Comiskey, Living Waters Conference (lecture, May 2004).

4. Mike Mason, *The Mystery of Marriage: Meditations on the Miracle*, 20th anniversary ed. (Sisters, OR: Multnomah, 2005), 70.

5. David G. Benner, *The Gift of Being Yourself: The Sacred Call to Self-Discovery* (Downers Grove, IL: InterVarsity Press, 2004), 92.

6. Timothy Keller with Kathy Keller, *The Meaning of Marriage: Facing the Complexities of Commitment with the Wisdom of God* (New York: Penguin Group, 2011), 17.

CHAPTER 2: NOT YOUR MOTHER'S LASAGNA

1. Marshall H. Klaus, John H. Kennell, and Phyllis H. Klaus, *Bonding: Building the Foundations of Secure Attachment and Independence* (Boston: Addison-Wesley, 1995), 48–49.

2. Klaus, Kennell, and Klaus, *Bonding*, 79–80.

CHAPTER 3: BEYOND PINK AND BLUE

1. Carolyn Custis James, *Malestrom: Manhood Swept into the Currents of a Changing World* (Grand Rapids, MI: Zondervan, 2015), 52.

2. Christopher adds these thoughts: In our experience walking with people who have significant internal conflicts regarding their gender identity, these extremes seem to be two sides of the same shame-based coin. Many aspects of gender nonconformity are normative and are to be embraced for both men and women, but this does not mean that one ever stops being one's birth gender with its physiological and cultural ramifications. If we cannot make peace within ourselves on this point, it can be very difficult to encounter a marital partner without significant turbulence or without losing a sense of personal identity. Gender rigidity within a culture can contribute to gender elasticity within particular individuals who don't measure up or have unresolved vulnerabilities within their gender identity. When this is the case, great compassion and wisdom are called for. There is no room for glibness, one-size-fits-all prescriptions, and condemnation. A safe and satisfying marriage may be the most favorable context in which to work out these delicate matters. Capable pastoral and clinical support may also be necessary.

3. Debra Hirsch, *Redeeming Sex: Naked Conversations about Sexuality and Spirituality* (Downers Grove, IL: InterVarsity Press, 2015), 89.

4. Mark A. Yarhouse, *Understanding Gender Dysphoria: Navigating Transgender Issues in a Changing Culture* (Downers Grove, IL: InterVarsity Press, 2015), 16–17.

5. Robert Gagnon, "The Old Testament and Homosexuality: A Critical Review of the Case Made by Phyllis Bird," www.robgagnon.net/articles/homosexBirdZAWarticle.pdf, 21–23.

6. Suzanne Burden, Carla Sunberg, and Jamie Wright, *Reclaiming Eve: The Identity and Calling of Women in the Kingdom of God* (Kansas City, MO: Beacon Hill Press, 2014), 25.

7. Burden, Sunberg, and Wright, *Reclaiming Eve*, 26.

8. See Andrew Comiskey, *Strength in Weakness: Overcoming Sexual and Relational Brokenness* (Downers Grove, IL: InterVarsity Press, 2003), 36–38.

9. Timothy Keller with Kathy Keller, *The Meaning of Marriage: Facing the Complexities of Commitment with the Wisdom of God* (New York: Penguin Group, 2011), 206.

10. Brené Brown, *I Thought It Was Just Me (But It Isn't): Making the Journey from "What Will People Think?" to "I Am Enough"* (New York: Gotham Books, 2007), 5.

11. Keller, *Meaning of Marriage*, 210.

12. Carolyn Custis James, *The Gospel of Ruth: Loving God Enough to Break the Rules* (Grand Rapids, MI: Zondervan, 2008), 101.

13. James, *The Gospel of Ruth*, 146.

14. James, *Malestrom*, 128.

15. James, *Malestrom*, 176.

CHAPTER 4: AN UNLIKELY BLESSING

1. See Gary Chapman, *The Five Love Languages: How to Express Heartfelt Commitment to Your Mate* (Chicago: Northfield, 1992).

2. Mike Mason, *The Mystery of Marriage: Meditations on the Miracle*, 20th anniversary ed. (Sisters, OR: Multnomah, 2005), 26.

3. Dr. Jeff Bjorck, clinical psychologist and professor at Fuller Seminary's Graduate School of Psychology, email message to author, December 2, 2015.

4. Bjorck, email message to author, December 2, 2015.

5. The idea of disordered desires or disordered attachments is from St. Ignatius and can be found in his writings, as well as those of St. Augustine, such as *Confessions*.

6. Dan Allender and Tremper Longman III, *The Cry of the Soul: How Our Emotions Reveal Our Deepest Questions about God* (Colorado Springs, CO: NavPress, 1994), 23.

7. Sarah Sumner, *Angry Like Jesus: Using His Example to Spark Your Moral Courage* (Minneapolis: Fortress, 2015), 3.

8. W. Robert Nay, *The Anger Management Workbook: Use the STOP Method to Replace Destructive Responses with Constructive Behavior* (New York: Guilford Press, 2014), 28.

9. Harriet Lerner, *The Dance of Anger: A Woman's Guide to Changing the Patterns of Intimate Relationships* (New York: Harper & Row, 1985), 1.

10. Allender and Longman, *Cry of the Soul*, 75–76.

11. Sumner, *Angry Like Jesus,* 20.

12. See Curt Thompson, *Anatomy of the Soul: Surprising Connections between Neuroscience and Spiritual Practices That Can Transform Your Life and Relationships* (Carol Stream, IL: Tyndale, 2010), 171–72, 197.

13. Jen Pollock Michel, *Teach Us to Want: Longing, Ambition and the Life of Faith* (Downers Grove, IL: InterVarsity Press, 2014), 43.

14. Michel, *Teach Us to Want*, 73.

CHAPTER 5: TUNING IN

1. Ann Voskamp, "3 Marriage Habits Every Marriage Needs—Because It's Worth Falling in Love Again," *A Holy Experience* (blog), January 9, 2013, www.aholyexperience.com/2013/01/3-marriage-habits-every-marriage -needs-to-fall-in-love-again/.

2. Adam McHugh, *The Listening Life: Embracing Attentiveness in a World of Distraction* (Downers Grove, IL: InterVarsity Press, 2015), 19, 81–82.

3. Gordon T. Smith, *Called to Be Saints: An Invitation to Christian Maturity* (Downers Grove, IL: InterVarsity Press, 2015), 139.

4. Richard C. Huseman, James M. Lahiff, and John M. Penrose, *Business Communication: Strategies and Skills* (Chicago: Dryden, 1991), 419.

5. Amanda Lenhart, "Cell Phones and American Adults," *Pew Research Center*, September 2, 2010, www.pewinternet.org/2010/09/02/cell-phones-and -american-adults/.

6. Sherry Turkle, "The Flight from Conversation," *New York Times*, April 21, 2012, www.nytimes.com/2012/04/22/opinion/sunday/the-flight-from -conversation.html?_r=0.

7. Sherry Turkle, *Alone Together: Why We Expect More from Technology and Less from Each Other* (New York: Basic Books, 2011), 12.

8. Gary Chapman, *The Five Love Languages: How to Express Heartfelt Commitment to Your Mate* (Chicago: Northfield, 1992), 63.

9. McHugh, *Listening Life*, 47.

10. Douglas Stone, Bruce Patton, and Sheila Heen, "Sort Out the Three Conversations," chap. 1 in *Difficult Conversations: How to Discuss What Matters Most* (New York: Penguin Books, 2000), 7–8.

CHAPTER 6: UNMASKING COUNTERFEITS

1. Gerald May, *Addiction and Grace: Love and Spirituality in the Healing of Addictions* (New York: Harper One, 1988), 3.

2. N. T. Wright, *Simply Christian: Why Christianity Makes Sense* (New York: HarperCollins, 2006), 209.

3. David Platt, *Counter Culture: A Compassionate Call to Counter Culture in a World of Poverty, Same-Sex Marriage, Racism....* (Carol Stream, IL: Tyndale, 2015), 159.

4. Based on a thorough reading of the Old Testament, the New Testament, and the history of Pauline doctrine, I have come to understand that sexual sin includes lust, genital sex outside of a heterosexual marriage, adultery, and prostitution.

5. May, *Addiction and Grace*, 14.

6. Craig R. Lockwood, *Falling Forward: The Pursuit of Sexual Purity* (Grandview, MO: Desert Stream Ministries, 2000), 2.

7. Patrick Carnes, *Out of the Shadows: Understanding Sexual Addiction*, 3rd ed. (Center City, MN: Hazelden, 2001), 8.

8. The last four stages were adapted from Carnes, *Out of the Shadows*, 19–20.

9. Danielle M. Dick, and Arpana Agrawal, "The Genetics of Alcohol and Other Drug Dependence," National Institute on Alcohol Abuse and Alcoholism, pubs.niaaa.nih.gov/publications/arh312/111-118.pdf.

10. Lockwood, *Falling Forward*, 118.

11. Those of you who have adult children who struggle with addiction, please know I write this in an attempt to help us understand the genesis of our addictions, not to blame you for your children's weaknesses. For more on this topic, see John Bowlby's *The Making and Breaking of Affectional Bonds* (New York: Routledge Classics, 2005).

12. Carnes, *Out of the Shadows*, 148.

13. Jan LaRue, "Senate Subcommittee Hears Experts on Pornography Toxicity," *Dr. Judith Reisman*, December 2, 2004, www.drjudithreisman.com /archives/2005/12/senate_subcommi.html.

14. Brother Lawrence, *The Practice of the Presence of God*, trans. E. M. Blaiklock (Nashville: Thomas Nelson, 1982), 53.

15. C. S. Lewis, from *The Weight of Glory* and Other Addresses, in *The Essential C. S. Lewis*, ed. Lyle Dorsett (New York: MacMillan, 1988), 362.

16. Such as Covenant Eyes, X3watch, or Net Nanny.

17. Gary Thomas, *The Glorious Pursuit: Embracing the Virtues of Christ* (Colorado Springs, CO: NavPress, 1998), 82.

18. May, *Addiction and Grace*, 13.

CHAPTER 7: NONNEGOTIABLES

1. Soong-Chan Rah, *Prophetic Lament: A Call for Justice in Troubled Times* (Downers Grove, IL: InterVarsity Press, 2015), 131.

2. Paul David Tripp, *What Did You Expect? Redeeming the Realities of Marriage* (Wheaton, IL: Crossway, 2010), 72.

3. Paul and Virginia Friesen, *The Marriage App: Unlocking the Irony of Intimacy* (Bedford, MA: Home Improvement Ministries, 2013), 175.

4. The encouragement to confess sins to one another is based on the assumption that both husband and wife are mature, faith-filled individuals able to hear a confession and understand how to respond with grace and mercy. If you are married to an unbeliever or if being honest might result in any form of violence, either verbal or physical, I would counsel you to find a healthy, same-gendered friend and confess to him or her. Domestic violence can be described as an ongoing pattern of coercion, intimidation, and/or emotional abuse, reinforced by the use and threat of physical or sexual violence. Please immediately seek out professional help if you or your children are in danger. See The National Domestic Violence Hotline (www.thehotline.org /is-this-abuse/abuse-defined); the Duluth Model (www.theduluthmodel .org); and Mary DeMuth's website, www.marydemuth.com.

5. Henri Nouwen, *The Road to Daybreak: A Spiritual Journey* (New York: Doubleday, 1988), 68.

6. "Forgiveness: Letting Go of Grudges and Bitterness," Mayo Clinic, November 11, 2014, www.mayoclinic.org/healthy-lifestyle/adult-health/in-depth /forgiveness/art-20047692.

7. Leslie Leyland Fields and Jill Hubbard, *Forgiving Our Mothers and Fathers: Finding Freedom from Hurt and Hate* (Nashville: Thomas Nelson, 2014), 96.

8. Fields and Hubbard, *Forgiving Our Mothers and Fathers*, 189.

CHAPTER 8: A PARADOX

1. Bronwyn Lea, "One Little Word That Radically Changed My Prayers," *Bronwyn Lea: Fueled by Grace, Caffeine and Laughter* (blog), August 6, 2013, bronlea.com/2013/08/06/one-little-word-that-radically-changed -my-prayers/.

2. Jerry Sittser, *A Grace Disguised: How the Soul Grows through Loss* (Grand Rapids, MI: Zondervan, 2004), 105.

3. C. S. Lewis, *The Problem of Pain* (New York: HarperCollins, 1996), 105.

4. Alexis de Tocqueville, quoted in Timothy Keller, *Walking with God through Pain and Suffering* (New York: Riverhead, 2013), 76.

5. C. Christopher Smith and John Pattison, *Slow Church: Cultivating Community in the Patient Way of Jesus* (Downers Grove, IL: InterVarsity Press, 2014), 63.

6. Keller, *Walking with God*, 21.

7. Keller, *Walking with God*, 23.

8. Keller, *Walking with God*, 49.

9. Sheli Geoghan-Massie, personal exchange with the author.

10. Michelle Van Loon, *If Only: Letting Go of Regret* (Kansas City, MO: Beacon Hill Press, 2014), 69.

11. Sittser, *A Grace Disguised*, 104.

12. Ann Voskamp, *One Thousand Gifts: A Dare to Live Fully Right Where You Are* (Grand Rapids, MI: Zondervan, 2010), 154–55.

13. Marlena Graves, *A Beautiful Disaster: Finding Hope in the Midst of Brokenness* (Grand Rapids, MI: Brazos, 2014), 94.

14. Lewis, *Problem of Pain*, 91.

15. *Ezer* is a Hebrew word that "appears twenty-one times in the Old Testament. Twice, in Genesis, it describes the woman (Gen. 2:18, 20). But the majority of references (sixteen to be exact) refer to God, or Yahweh, as the helper of his people.… If language means anything, the *ezer*, in every case, is … a very *strong* helper." Carolyn Custis James, *When Life and Beliefs Collide: How Knowing God Makes a Difference* (Grand Rapids, MI: Zondervan, 2001), 181.

16. Lewis, *Problem of Pain*, 34, 41.

CHAPTER 9: CHOOSING JOY

1. Margaret Feinberg, *Fight Back with Joy: Celebrate More. Regret Less. Stare Down Your Greatest Fears.* (Brentwood, TN: Worthy Books, 2015), 19.

2. Feinberg, *Fight Back*, 85–87.

3. Feinberg, *Fight Back*, 19.

4. Jerry Sittser, *A Grace Disguised: How the Soul Grows through Loss* (Grand Rapids, MI: Zondervan, 2004), 48.

5. Feinberg, *Fight Back*, 79.

6. Amy Simpson, *Anxious: Choosing Faith in a World of Worry* (Downers Grove, IL: InterVarsity Press, 2014), 46, 48.

7. C. Christopher Smith and John Pattison, *Slow Church: Cultivating Community in the Patient Way of Jesus* (Downers Grove, IL: InterVarsity Press, 2014), 184.

8. Jen Pollock Michel, *Teach Us to Want: Longing, Ambition and the Life of Faith* (Downers Grove, IL: InterVarsity Press, 2014), 119–20.

9. Feinberg, *Fight Back*, 23.

CHAPTER 10: IT'S NOT GOOD TO BE ALONE

1. C. Christopher Smith and John Pattison, *Slow Church: Cultivating Community in the Patient Way of Jesus* (Downers Grove, IL: InterVarsity Press, 2014), 33.

2. Dietrich Bonhoeffer, *Life Together* (New York: Harper & Brothers, 1954), 26–27, 30.

3. *The Book of Common Prayer* (New York: Church Publishing Incorporated), www.episcopalchurch.org/files/book_of_common_prayer.pdf, 425.

4. Andrew Comiskey, *Living Waters* (Grandview, MO: Desert Stream Press, 2000), 103.

5. Jonathan Wilson-Hartgrove, *The Wisdom of Stability: Rooting Faith in a Mobile Culture* (Brewster, MA: Paraclete, 2010), 21.

6. Wilson-Hartgrove, *Wisdom of Stability*, 39.

CHAPTER 11: MADE BEAUTIFUL

1. Gary Thomas, *Sacred Marriage* (Grand Rapids, MI: Zondervan, 2000), 108.

2. Marlena Graves, *A Beautiful Disaster: Finding Hope in the Midst of Brokenness* (Grand Rapids, MI: Brazos, 2014), 56.

3. Andrea Palpant Dilley, *Faith and Other Flat Tires: Searching for God on the Rough Road of Doubt* (Grand Rapids, MI: Zondervan, 2012), 235.

4. Mike Mason, *The Mystery of Marriage: Meditations on the Miracle*, 20th anniversary ed. (Sisters, OR: Multnomah, 2005), 151.

5. Mason, *Mystery of Marriage*, 151.

6. Audrey Assad, "The Key to Our Joy," *Mudroom: Making Room in the Mess* (blog), November 24, 2015, mudroomblog.com/the-key-to-our-joy/.

7. Luci Shaw, "Bloodline," in Sarah Arthur, *Between Midnight and Dawn: A Literary Guide to Prayer for Lent, Holy Week, and Eastertide* (Brewster, MA: Paraclete, 2016), 184.

8. Francis Chan and Lisa Chan, *You and Me Forever: Marriage in Light of Eternity* (San Francisco: Claire Love, 2014), 9, 113.

ABOUT THE AUTHOR

For more than twenty years, Dorothy Greco and her husband, Christopher, have helped couples create and sustain healthy marriages. Dorothy has written for *Relevant* magazine; *Sojourners*; Christianity Today's *Her.meneutics*, *Today's Christian Woman*, and *Gifted for Leadership*; StartMarriageRight.com; SheLovesMagazine.com; and many others. She has also worked as a professional photographer for more than thirty years. Dorothy and Christopher recently celebrated their twenty-fifth wedding anniversary. They have three sons and one daughter-in-law.

To connect with Dorothy and find a small-group study guide and a supplementary reading list, please visit her website at www.dorothygreco.com. You can also follow her on social media:

Facebook: Words & Images by Dorothy Greco

(www.facebook.com/dorothygrecophotography)

Twitter: @dorothygreco

Instagram: @dorothylgreco